Earl Nightingale - On Success

CONTENTS

Earl Nightingale - On Success 3

About The Author...8

Chapter 1
 The Strangest Secret..10

Chapter 2
 Follow Your River...22

Chapter 3
 The River or the Goal...25

Chapter 4
 How to React to Stress...28

Chapter 5
 Life of the Unsuccessful...30

Chapter 6
 Six Techniques for Creative Revolutions....................................33

Chapter 7
 The Devil's Wedge...39

Chapter 8
 The Profile of a Creative Person...42

Chapter 9
 A Commitment to Laughter...46

Chapter 10
A Time to Risk or Sit...49

Chapter 11
The Entrepreneurial Adventure...51

Chapter 12
The Cure for Procrastination..56

Chapter 13
The Great Problem-Solving Tool..59

Chapter 14
Is Your Personal Corporation Growing?...................................64

Chapter 15
Falling Isn't Failing..66

Chapter 16
The $25,000 Idea..68

Chapter 1 7
The Fog of Worry 73

Chapter 18
The Boss...75

Chapter 19
What Is Your Intermediate Goal?...83

Chapter 20
Success: A Worthy Destination..85

Chapter 21
Fake It Till You Make It...92

Chapter 22
It's Not the Destination...95

Chapter 23
Acres of Diamonds...97

Chapter 24
Don't Follow the Follower...104

Chapter 25
The Difference Between the 'Haves' & the 'Have Nots'...........107

Chapter 26
The Flame of Hope...112

Chapter 27
Nine Steps for Solving Any Problem..........................114

Chapter 28
A Pain in the Colon...119

Chapter 29
Lloyd Conant: This I Believe.....................................121

Chapter 30
Is Your Destination Clear?..130

Chapter 31
What Happens When You Run Out of Goals?...............136

Chapter 32
Napoleon Hill's Think and Grow Rich.......................138

Chapter 33
How to Give a Great Speech......................................150

About The Author

As a Depression-era child, Earl Nightingale was hungry for knowledge. From the time he was a young boy, he would frequent the Long Beach Public Library in California, searching for the answer to the question, "How can a person, starting from scratch, who has no particular advantage in the world, reach the goals that he feels are important to him, and by so doing, make a major contribution to others?" His desire to find an answer, coupled with his natural curiosity about the world and its workings, spurred him to become one of the world's foremost experts on success and what makes people successful.

Earl Nightingale's early career began when, as a member of the Marine Corps, he volunteered to work at a local radio station as an announcer. The Marines also gave him a chance to travel, although he only got as far as Hawaii when the Japanese attacked Pearl Harbor in 1941. Earl managed to be one of the few survivors aboard the battleship Arizona. After five more years in the service, Earl and his wife moved first to Phoenix then Chicago to build what was to be a very fruitful career in network radio.

As the host of his own daily commentary program on WGN, Earl Nightingale arranged a deal that also gave him a commission on his own advertising sales. By 1957, he was so successful he decided to retire at the age of 35. In the meantime, Earl had bought his own insurance company and had spent many hours motivating its sales force to greater accomplishments. When he decided to go on vacation for an extended period of time, his sales manager begged him to put his inspirational words on record. The result later became the recording entitled The Strangest Secret, the first spoken word message to win a Gold Record by selling over a million copies.

In The Strangest Secret, Earl had found an answer to the question that had inspired him as a youth and, in turn, found a way to leave a lasting legacy for others. About this time, Earl met a successful businessman by the name of Lloyd Conant and together they began an "electronic publishing" company which eventually grew to become a multi-million dollar giant in the self-improvement field. They also developed a syndicated, 5-minute daily radio program, Our Changing World, which became the longest-running, most widely syndicated show in radio.

When Earl Nightingale died on March 28, 1989, Paul Harvey broke the news to the country on his radio program with the words, "The sonorous voice of the nightingale was stilled." In the words of his good friend and commercial announcer, Steve King, "Earl Nightingale never let a day go by that he didn't learn something new and, in turn, pass it on to others. It was his consuming passion."

Chapter 1

The Strangest Secret

This amazing message was first played for a group of salespeople at Earl Nightingale's insurance agency. They were utterly electrified. Word of it spread like wildfire, and everyone who heard it was positively ignited into action. Requests for a recording of the message came pouring in - thousands of requests per week. Within no time, more than 200,000 people had called, written, or just walked right into Earl's office to request a copy. As years went by, that number soared above 1,000,000.

By 1956, Earl Nightingale had already soared to successful heights as a Network radio announcer: the voice of Sky King; and host of his own daily radio and television show. Expanding his horizon, he bought a small Life Insurance company, insuring it's success by giving encouraging, inspiring, motivational talks to his sales staff. Then because he was going to be away, Earl wrote and recorded on a record, an essay which could be played during his absence. He called it THE STRANGEST SECRET. The response to the message had such an impact on the staff that requests for copies to share with friends and families grew. Columbia Records filled the requests and within a short period of time sales soared to over a million copies, earning a Gold Record - the first and only spoken word record to ever read Gold!

Today, more than 40 years later, *The Strangest Secret* remains one of the most powerful and influential messages ever recorded. It continues to transform the lives of everyone who hears and heeds it.
Prescription for success: listen or read twice a month for the next ten years, then once a month forever.

The Strangest Secret

Know what will happen to 100 individuals who start even at the age of 25, and who believe they will be successful? By the age of 65, only five out of 100 will make the grade! Why do so many fail? What happened to the sparkle that was there when they were 25? What became of their dreams, their hopes, their plans... and why is there such a large disparity between what theses people intended to do and what they actually accomplished? That is... The Strangest Secret.

Some years ago, the late Nobel prize-winning Dr. Albert Schweitzer was asked by a reporter, "Doctor, what's wrong with men today? The great doctor was silent a moment, and then he said, "Men simply don't think!"

It's about this that I want to talk with you. We live today in a golden age. This is an era that humanity has looked forward to, dreamed of, and worked toward for thousands of years. We live in the richest era that ever existed on the face of the earth... a land of abundant opportunity for everyone.

However, if you take 100 individuals who start even at the age of 25, do you have any idea what will happen to those men and women by the time they're 65? These 100 people believe they're going to be successful. They are eager toward life, there is a certain sparkle in their eye, an erectness to their carriage, and life seems like a pretty interesting adventure to them.

But by the time they're 65, only one will be rich, four will be financially independent, five will still be working, and 54 will be broke - depending on others for life's necessities.

Only five out of 100 make the grade! Why do so many fail? What has happened to the sparkle that was there when they were 25? What has become of the dreams, the hopes, the plans... and why is there such a large disparity between what these people intended to do and what they actually accomplished?

THE DEFINITION OF SUCCESS

First, we have to define success and here is the best definition I've ever been able to find: "Success is the progressive realization of a worthy ideal."

A success is the schoolteacher who is teaching because that's what he or she wants to do. A success is the entrepreneur who started his own company because that was his dream - that's what he wanted to do. A success is the salesperson who wants to become the best salesperson in his or her company and sets forth on the pursuit of that goal.

A success is anyone who is realizing a worthy predetermined ideal, because that's what he or she decided to do... deliberately. But only one out of 20 does that! The rest are "failures."

Rollo May, the distinguished psychiatrist, wrote a wonderful book called Man's Search for Himself, and in this book he says: "The opposite of courage in our society is not cowardice... it is conformity." And there you have the reason for so many failures. Conformity - people acting like everyone else, without knowing why or where they are going.

We learn to read by the time we're seven. We learn to make a living by the time we're 30. Often by that time we're not only

making a living, we're supporting a family. And yet by the time we're 65, we haven't learned how to become financially independent in the richest land that has ever been known. Why? We conform! Most of us are acting like the wrong percentage group - the 95 who don't succeed.

GOALS

Have you ever wondered why so many people work so hard and honestly without ever achieving anything in particular, and why others don't seem to work hard, yet seem to get everything? They seem to have the "magic touch." You've heard people say, "Everything he touches turns to gold." Have you ever noticed that a person who becomes successful tends to continue to become more successful? And, on the other hand, have you noticed how someone who's a failure tends to continue to fail?

The difference is goals. People with goals succeed because they know where they're going. It's that simple. Failures, on the other hand, believe that their lives are shaped by circumstances... by things that happen to them... by exterior forces.

Think of a ship with the complete voyage mapped out and planned. The captain and crew know exactly where the ship is going and how long it will take - it has a definite goal. And 9,999 times out of 10,000, it will get there.

Now let's take another ship - just like the first - only let's not put a crew on it, or a captain at the helm. Let's give it no aiming point, no goal, and no destination. We just start the engines and let it go. I think you'll agree that if it gets out of the harbor at all, it will either sink or wind up on some deserted

beach - a derelict. It can't go anyplace because it has no destination and no guidance.

It's the same with a human being. However, the human race is fixed, not to prevent the strong from winning, but to prevent the weak from losing. Society today can be likened to a convoy in time of war. The entire society is slowed down to protect its weakest link, just as the naval convoy has to go at the speed that will permit its slowest vessel to remain in formation.

That's why it's so easy to make a living today. It takes no particular brains or talent to make a living and support a family today. We have a plateau of so-called "security." So, to succeed, all we must do is decide how high above this plateau we want to aim.

Throughout history, the great wise men and teachers, philosophers, and prophets have disagreed with one another on many different things. It is only on this one point that they are in complete and unanimous agreement - the key to success and the key to failure is this:

WE BECOME WHAT WE THINK ABOUT

This is The Strangest Secret! Now, why do I say it's strange, and why do I call it a secret? Actually, it isn't a secret at all. It was first promulgated by some of the earliest wise men, and it appears again and again throughout the Bible. But very few people have learned it or understand it. That's why it's strange, and why for some equally strange reason it virtually remains a secret.

Marcus Aurelius, the great Roman Emperor, said: "A man's life is what his thoughts make of it."

Disraeli said this: "Everything comes if a man will only wait... a human being with a settled purpose must accomplish it, and nothing can resist a will that will stake even existence for its fulfillment."

William James said: "We need only in cold blood act as if the thing in question were real, and it will become infallibly real by growing into such a connection with our life that it will become real. It will become so knit with habit and emotion that our interests in it will be those which characterize belief." He continues, "...only you must, then, really wish these things, and wish them exclusively, and not wish at the same time a hundred other incompatible things just as strongly."

My old friend Dr. Norman Vincent Peale put it this way: "If you think in negative terms, you will get negative results. If you think in positive terms, you will achieve positive results."

George Bernard Shaw said: "People are always blaming their circumstances for what they are. I don't believe in circumstances. The people who get on in this world are the people who get up and look for the circumstances they want, and if they can't find them, make them."

Well, it's pretty apparent, isn't it? We become what we think about. A person who is thinking about a concrete and worthwhile goal is going to reach it, because that's what he's thinking about. Conversely, the person who has no goal, who doesn't know where he's going, and whose thoughts must therefore be thoughts of confusion, anxiety, fear, and worry will thereby create a life of frustration, fear, anxiety and worry. And if he thinks about nothing... he becomes nothing.

AS YE SOW - SO SHALL YE REAP

The human mind is much like a farmer's land. The land gives the farmer a choice. He may plant in that land whatever he chooses. The land doesn't care what is planted. It's up to the farmer to make the decision. The mind, like the land, will return what you plant, but it doesn't care what you plant. If the farmer plants two seeds - one a seed of corn, the other nightshade, a deadly poison, waters and takes care of the land, what will happen?

Remember, the land doesn't care. It will return poison in just as wonderful abundance as it will corn. So up come the two plants - one corn, one poison as it's written in the Bible, "As ye sow, so shall ye reap."

The human mind is far more fertile, far more incredible and mysterious than the land, but it works the same way. It doesn't care what we plant... success... or failure. A concrete, worthwhile goal... or confusion, misunderstanding, fear, anxiety, and so on. But what we plant it must return to us.

The problem is that our mind comes as standard equipment at birth. It's free. And things that are given to us for nothing, we place little value on. Things that we pay money for, we value.

The paradox is that exactly the reverse is true. Everything that's really worthwhile in life came to us free - our minds, our souls, our bodies, our hopes, our dreams, our ambitions, our intelligence, our love of family and children and friends and country. All these priceless possessions are free.

But the things that cost us money are actually very cheap and can be replaced at any time. A good man can be completely wiped out and make another fortune. He can do that several times. Even if our home burns down, we can rebuild it. But the things we got for nothing, we can never replace.

Our mind can do any kind of job we assign to it, but generally speaking, we use it for little jobs instead of big ones. So decide now. What is it you want? Plant your goal in your mind. It's the most important decision you'll ever make in your entire life.

Do you want to excel at your particular job? Do you want to go places in your company... in your community? Do you want to get rich? All you have got to do is plant that seed in your mind, care for it, work steadily toward your goal, and it will become a reality.

It not only will, there's no way that it cannot. You see, that's a law - like the laws of Sir Isaac Newton, the laws of gravity. If you get on top of a building and jump off, you'll always go down - you'll never go up.

And it's the same with all the other laws of nature. They always work. They're inflexible. Think about your goal in a relaxed, positive way. Picture yourself in your mind's eye as having already achieved this goal. See yourself doing the things you will be doing when you have reached your goal.

Every one of us is the sum total of our own thoughts. We are where we are because that's exactly where we really want or feel we deserve to be - whether we'll admit that or not. Each of us must live off the fruit of our thoughts in the future, because what you think today and tomorrow - next month and next year - will mold your life and determine your future. You're guided by your mind.
I remember one time I was driving through eastern Arizona and I saw one of those giant earth-moving machines roaring

along the road with what looked like 30 tons of dirt in it - a tremendous, incredible machine - and there was a little man perched way up on top with the wheel in his hands, guiding it. As I drove along I was struck by the similarity of that machine to the human mind. Just suppose you're sitting at the controls of such a vast source of energy. Are you going to sit back and fold your arms and let it run itself into a ditch? Or are you going to keep both hands firmly on the wheel and control and direct this power to a specific, worthwhile purpose? It's up to you. You're in the driver's seat.

You see, the very law that gives us success is a double-edged sword. We must control our thinking. The same rule that can lead people to lives of success, wealth, happiness, and all the things they ever dreamed of - that very same law can lead them into the gutter. It's all in how they use it... for good or for bad. That is The Strangest Secret!

Do what the experts since the dawn of recorded history have told us to do: pay the price, by becoming the person you want to become. It's not nearly as difficult as living unsuccessfully.

The moment you decide on a goal to work toward, you're immediately a successful person - you are then in that rare group of people who know where they're going. Out of every hundred people, you belong to the top five. Don't concern yourself too much with how you are going to achieve your goal - leave that completely to a power greater than yourself. All you have to do is know where you're going. The answers will come to you of their own accord, and at the right time.

Start today. You have nothing to lose - but you have your whole life to win.

30-DAY ACTION IDEAS FOR PUTTING THE STRANGEST SECRET TO WORK FOR YOU

For the next 30-days follow each of these steps every day until you have achieved your goal.

1. Write on a card what it is you want more that anything else. It may be more money. Perhaps you'd like to double your income or make a specific amount of money. It may be a beautiful home. It may be success at your job. It may be a particular position in life. It could be a more harmonious family.

Write down on your card specifically what it is you want. Make sure it's a single goal and clearly defined. You needn't show it to anyone, but carry it with you so that you can look at it several times a day. Think about it in a cheerful, relaxed, positive way each morning when you get up, and immediately you have something to work for - something to get out of bed for, something to live for.

Look at it every chance you get during the day and just before going to bed at night. As you look at it, remember that you must become what you think about, and since you're thinking about your goal, you realize that soon it will be yours. In fact, it's really yours the moment you write it down and begin to think about it.

2. Stop thinking about what it is you fear. Each time a fearful or negative thought comes into your mind, replace it with a mental picture of your positive and worthwhile goal. And there will come a time when you'll feel like giving up. It's easier for a human being to think negatively than positively. That's why only five percent are successful! You must begin now to place yourself in that group.

"Act as though it were impossible to fail," as Dorothea Brande said. No matter what your goal - if you've kept your goal before you every day - you'll wonder and marvel at this new life you've found.

3. Your success will always be measured by the quality and quantity of service you render. Most people will tell you that they want to make money, without understanding this law. The only people who make money work in a mint. The rest of us must earn money. This is what causes those who keep looking for something for nothing, or a free ride, to fail in life. Success is not the result of making money; earning money is the result of success - and success is in direct proportion to our service.

Most people have this law backwards. It's like the man who stands in front of the stove and says to it: "Give me heat and then I'll add the wood." How many men and women do you know, or do you suppose there are today, who take the same attitude toward life? There are millions.

We've got to put the fuel in before we can expect heat. Likewise, we've got to be of service first before we can expect money. Don't concern yourself with the money. Be of service... build... work... dream... create! Do this and you'll find there is no limit to the prosperity and abundance that will come to you.

Don't start your test until you've made up your mind to stick with it. If you should fail during your first 30 days - by that I mean suddenly find yourself overwhelmed by negative thoughts - simply start over again from that point and go 30 more days. Gradually, your new habit will form, until you find yourself one of that wonderful minority to whom virtually nothing is impossible.

Above all... don't worry! Worry brings fear, and fear is crippling. The only thing that can cause you to worry during your test is trying to do it all yourself. Know that all you have to do is hold your goal before you; everything else will take care of itself.

Take this 30-day test, then repeat it... then repeat it again. Each time it will become more a part of you until you'll wonder how you could have ever have lived any other way. Live this new way and the floodgates of abundance will open and pour over you more riches than you may have dreamed existed. Money? Yes, lots of it. But what's more important, you'll have peace... you'll be in that wonderful minority who lead calm, cheerful, successful lives.

Start today. You have nothing to lose. But you have a life to win.

Chapter 2

Follow Your River

Are you immersed in your "river of interest" or simply watching your life from the shore... afraid to get your feet wet?

There are two distinct kinds of successful people. There are what I call the river people and the goal people. Let's take a good look at the river people. River people are those fortunate people who find themselves born to perform a special task. Mozart and da Vinci were river people. There are thousands of river people living today. They're the people who know from childhood what they want to do with their lives.

River people seem born to spend their lives in pursuit of their interest. And they throw themselves into their rivers 100 percent, busying themselves with whatever it happens to be. They don't tend to think about the idea of success or the making of money; they simply spend their lives doing the best they can in their river of interest. And they're often responsible for some of the largest achievements and institutions on earth.

We all know the stories of Alexander Graham Bell and Thomas Edison. The
businesses that have grown from their inventions encircle the globe and are among the largest on the planet. Einstein was such a person, of course, but there are thousands of them that we never hear of. They are people who would be perfectly content in their fields of interest with only a modest maintenance diet and a roof over their heads. Their work is everything. But because they usually render a very valuable service in the performance of their work, be it in the arts or sports or commerce, they're usually well rewarded for their

efforts, though they may struggle for years before recognition and success come to them.

Dr. Abraham Maslow talked about such people. He said, "One could say a good match is like the perfect love affair or friendship in which it seems that people belong to each other and were meant for each other. In the best instances, the person and his job fit together and belong together perfectly, like a key in a lock, or perhaps resonate together like a sung note which sits in a sympathetic resonance, a particular string on a piano keyboard." And Maslow said, "Simply as a matter of the strategy and tactics of living well and fully, and of choosing one's life instead of having it determined for us, this is a help."

It's so easy to forget ultimates in the rush and hurry of daily life, especially for young people. So often, we're merely responders, so to speak, simply reacting to stimuli, to rewards and punishments, to emergencies, to pains and fears, to demands of other people, to superficialities. It takes a specific, conscious effort, at least at first, to turn one's attention to intrinsic things and values. Perhaps seeking actual physical aloneness. Perhaps exposing one's self to great music, to good people, to natural beauty, and so forth. Only after practice do these strategies become easy and automatic so that one can be living totally immersed in his or her river.

I believe that each of us, because of the way our genetic heritage is stacked, has an area of great interest. And it's that area that we should explore with the patience and assiduity of a paleontologist on an important dig where it's a region of great potential. Somewhere within it, we can find that avenue of interest that so perfectly matches our natural abilities, we'll be able to make our greatest contribution and spend our lives in work we love.

If we can find our river of interest, we need only throw ourselves into it, fully committed, and there spend our days learning and growing and finding new emerging fields of interest within its boundaries.

Chapter 3

The River or the Goal

For some, the river may be a particular branch of science; for others, one of the arts. There are some physicians, for example, who are so wrapped up in medicine that they hate to leave; even after a 16-hour day, they can't wait to get back to it.

These people are happiest and most alive when they're in their river - in whatever business or career or profession it happens to be. And success comes to such people as inevitable as a sunrise. In fact, they are successes the moment they find their great field of interest; the worldly trappings of success will always come in time. Such people don't have to ask, "What will I do with my life?" *Their work is a magnet for them, and they can't imagine doing anything else.*

We all know such people, or about such people. Doing what they do is even more important to them than the rewards they earn for doing it.

The second group of successful people are those who are goal-oriented. These people have not found a particular river, necessarily, and can be quite happy doing a number of things. It's the goals they set that are important to them, and they're quite aware that there are many roads that can lead to their goals.

Someone once said, *'Americans can have anything they seriously make up their minds to have. The trouble is that most of them never make up their minds about anything."* Goal-oriented people do make up their minds about what they want, and they keep their eyes and their enthusiasm on the goal they've established until it becomes a reality in their lives. Then they set a new goal, if they're wise.

One of the problems with this latter group is that after achieving a number of goals and becoming quite successful, they can run out of goals and become listless and unhappy. But not the river people. Their interest in what they're doing never fades.

So if you're going to be a big success, chances are you need to be a river person or a goal-oriented person, or both - the two groups are not mutually exclusive.

Tips for Setting Goals

A clinical associate professor of psychiatry, Dr. Ari Kiev, writes, "Observing the lives of people who have mastered adversity, I have noted that they have established goals and sought with all their effort to achieve them. From the moment they decide to concentrate all their energies on a specific objective, they began to surmount the most difficult odds. "

Dr. Kiev continues, "The establishment of a goal is the key to successful living. And the most important step toward achieving an objective is first to define it. I'm sure you have at least 30 minutes a day in which to list your thoughts. At the end of that time, choose from the possible objectives you have listed, the one that seems the most important, and record it separately on a single card. Carry this card with you at all times. Think about this goal every day. Create a concrete mental image of the goal, as if you've already accomplished it.

The doctor points out, "You can determine your special talents or strengths in a number of ways, ranging from psychological tests to an analysis of the unexpressed wishes in your dreams.

No method works for everyone. You might start, for example, by clipping and posting newspaper articles that interest you. After 30 days, see if there isn't some trend suggestive or a deep-seated interest of natural inclination. Keep alert to the slightest indications of any special skills or talents, even when they seem silly or unimportant.

"From this exercise, you should be able to get some sense of potential strengths. Whenever you discover a strength or talent, think of five possible ways to develop it. Write these down on a card as well, and check them periodically to keep them fresh in your mind."

So take the good advice of psychiatrist Dr. Ari Kiev, and don't be afraid of failure. As Herodotus wrote, "It is better by noble boldness to run the risk of being subject to half of the evils we anticipate than to remain in cowardly listlessness for fear of what may happen. "

Chapter 4

How to React to Stress

Two young boys were raised by an alcoholic father. As they grew older, they moved away from that broken home, each going his own way in the world. Several years later, they happened to be interviewed separately by a psychologist who was analyzing the effects of drunkenness on children in broken homes. His research revealed that the two men were strikingly different from each other. One was a clean-living teetotaler; the other, a hopeless drunk like his father. The psychologist asked each of them why he developed the way he did, and each gave an identical answer, "What else would you expect when you have a father like mine?"

That story was revealed by Dr. Hans Selye, internationally renowned Canadian physician and scientist known as the father of stress. A medical pioneer, he devoted the majority of his years to the exploration of biological stress. And he related the story of the two sons of the drunken father in an article for *New Realities.*

And the story demonstrates a cardinal rule implicit in stress, health, and human behavior. According to R. H. Schuller, "It is not what happens to you in life that makes the difference. It is how you react to each circumstance you encounter that determines the result. Every human being in the same situation has the possibilities of choosing how he will react - either positively or negatively."

Thus, stress is not necessarily caused by stressor agents; rather, it is caused by the way stressor agents are perceived, interpreted, or appraised in each individual case. Outside events and people upset some more than others, because they are looked upon and dealt with in entirely different ways. The stressors may even be the same in each case, yet the reaction will almost always be different in different people.

Armed with that kind of information, it would seem that we can greatly improve our reactions to stressful situations. What seems to be a cruel world to one person might be filled with challenge and opportunity to another. It is our reaction that makes the difference.

Chapter 5

Life of the Unsuccessful

What separates the unsuccessful from the successful?

When I think about unsuccessful people, I think of those men and women who seem to be at the mercy of forces over which they seem helpless or uninterested in influencing. I was raised as a boy in such circumstances and came to know them well. I watched people who seemed helpless to do anything about their problems. Their most serious shortcoming was of course lack of education. They took their cues from those about them, which is the self-defeating cycle of the poor - they're always following the wrong group.

More than any other factor, perhaps, the unsuccessful person can usually be identified with a group that is at the mercy of events. The unsuccessful person has things done to him or her. The successful person seeks autonomy and makes his or her own plans and has the self-esteem and inner excitement and knowledge to know that those plans can be followed, barring a calamity over which he or she can exercise no control. The unsuccessful person tends to focus on the calamity or ride with the punches. The successful person gives; the unsuccessful person takes. But since we cannot reap more than we sow, the unsuccessful person, sowing little, reaps little.

Have you ever heard someone say, "I do no more than I'm paid to do." Sure, we all have. And that person has stuck himself in a no-win fix. Doing no more than he's paid to do, that man can never earn more than he's receiving, other than just cost-of-living raises. He is an unsuccessful man. His attitude has got him stuck in a corner, and until or unless something changes it, in that corner, he's going to remain. There's nothing at all that unsuccessful people have or do that successful people do not have more of and do better.

Unsuccessful people are not stronger or in better physical condition than successful people. They're not better parents, wives, or husbands. About the only thing you can say about the unsuccessful is, as the well-known saying has it, God must have loved them. He made so many of them.

The word *poor* still applies to far too many human beings in the United States. I keep hearing politicians say that we still have not reached the proper distribution of income. But income is not a factor of distribution; income is *earned* by someone. If it is given to the poor, as it should be, it's because it was earned by someone else. A country as rich as the United States should have a level of subsystems below which no one should be permitted to fall. But what is needed most is the kind of education calculated to help people help themselves. And for those who cannot help themselves - the old, the sick, the incompetent - subsistence and clean, healthful surroundings should be one of our most important national goals.

But the unsuccessful serve in one important way. We need the millions of unsuccessful people from whose ranks we can recruit the successful people of the future. Where do you think successful people come from? That's right, they come from unsuccessful people. They are each an original, never before seen upon planet earth, with deep abilities and talents just lying dormant, waiting for the fertilization, the irrigation of good ideas and enthusiasm to get them started growing.

Even her Royal Highness, the Queen of England, had unsuccessful ancestors, if you go back far enough. As human creatures, we all started even somewhere in time. And for every successful family, there was someone who had the drive, ambition, and determination to break from the crowd and start the ball rolling... to free himself from the ranks of the unsuccessful and venture into the camp of the successful.

Chapter 6

Six Techniques for Creative Revolutions

To spur your mind to new action, think combination, adaptation, substitution, magnification, minification, and rearrangement.

What are some of the best techniques for using our creative faculties more effectively to solve problems, make decisions, achieve goals, and better fulfill our ultimate human responsibility, which is to think? Here are a few I have learned:

Think Combination

Everything you see, hear, touch, taste, and smell during the day offers you the opportunity to consider new combinations. When you brush your teeth, you might think of a toothbrush that contains the toothpaste in the handle. You might combine your mirror with a motto reminding you to start the day right. It might read, "How can I increase my service today?" or "Have no small dreams!" That's thinking combination. A simple pencil is a combination of wood, carbon, rubber, paint, and metal. You can come up with great ideas that can lead to profits, patents, and even billion-dollar companies by finding new combinations yourself. Here are a few ways entrepreneurs have profited from thinking combination.

A French company invented an ordinary snorkel combined with a radio - the first battery-powered snorkel with an FM radio receiver built in, and it doesn't even require an earpiece. The product, AQUA FM, uses unique bone conduction technology to transmit sound through the teeth and into the inner ear, providing clear, amazing sound.

In another example, companies like Vonage and Skype have revolutionized telephone service by combining a telephone and the Internet, and the big telecom companies are clambering to keep up. Telephone companies have always charged by the minute for long distance services, but the Internet is different. Broadband is charged at a standard monthly rate for unlimited use. VOIP (Voice over IP) start-up companies have used this to their advantage and thought differently about telephone service. Why pay by the minute to send data via your telephone service when you have a data tunnel you are already paying for - your broadband connection? Simply piggyback on that by connecting your phone to your broadband and talk to anyone in the world for a fraction of the cost.

Think Adaptation

Velcro was created through adaptation. In 1948, George de Mestral, a Swiss engineer, returned from a walk through a field of weeds one day and found some cockleburs [burrs] clinging to his cloth jacket. After studying one of the cockleburs under a microscope, he noticed it was a maze of thin strands with burrs (or hooks) on the ends that cling to fabrics or animal fur. He then recognized the potential for a practical new fastener. It took eight years to experiment, develop, and perfect the invention, but now Velcro is a well-known, incredibly useful product. Velcro has even been further adapted for making all kinds of products better - from shoes that use Velcro instead of laces, to adjustable Velcro wrist straps on boxing gloves.

In another example, designers took tiny flexible optical fibers developed for high-energy physics experiments and wove them into ordinary fabric. This adaptation created a new fabric called Luminex that glows, literally. It's not shiny and it's not glow in the dark; it gives off its own light. Now Luminex is being used in stage costumes, handbags, and curtains as well as clothing.

During the next year you are going to see the result of people thinking adaptation and coming up with ideas worth millions of dollars. Why couldn't one of these people be you? The only limit to what you can achieve by adapting old products to new uses - old methods to new applications - is the limit of your own creativity.

Think Substitution

When you think substitution, ask yourself how you might substitute a different idea, product, or material for the one now used. For example, soy burgers are the vegetarian's substitute for meat products.

And plastic lumber is now used as a substitute for concrete, wood, and metals. Yes, recycled plastic lumber (RPL) is a wood-like product made from recovered plastic or recovered plastic mixed with other materials. This plastic lumber can then be transformed by consumers and manufacturers into a wide range of products, including decks and docks, landscape timbers, parking stops, picnic tables, benches, trash receptacles, planters, and numerous custom applications (think adaptation!).

You can also take an existing product and make it better through thinking substitution. Take, for instance, luggage with wheels. This was a wonderful invention because it eliminated the need to carry luggage. But, for years the wheels were made of cheap plastic, often only a step better than dragging your luggage on the ground. It wasn't until recently that someone decided to replace these cheap plastic wheels with the high-speed ball-bearing efficient wheels from Rollerblade skates.

This substitution created a better-wheeled suitcase and made for happier travelers.

In short, don't assume because a particular thing has always been used in the past, that you have to use it now. Perhaps there's a substitution that will work better or last longer, or cost less, or be lighter, or more colorful, and so forth. Think substitution.

Think magnification

Think big! Examples include skyscrapers, the Pentagon, king-size soft drinks, and the IMAX theatre. IMAX was started by Canadian filmmakers/entrepreneurs who wanted bigger and better theaters. Now IMAX is the ultimate movie experience, helping people see more, feel more, and hear more.

Vehicles are getting bigger, too. We've had trucks and vans for many years. But in recent years soccer dads and carpool moms have demanded a different large vehicle - the SUV. The Hummer, Lincoln Navigator, Cadillac Escalade, and Suburban are just a few of the behemoths that safely courier our children to and from their daily activities.

Yet, while most car companies are going larger, BMW went the opposite way, which takes us to our next thinking strategy...

Think Minification

Think small! In the midst of the SUV explosion, BMW was thinking small and acquired the rights to the Mini Cooper. This just proves that magnification and minification can succeed in the same market concurrently.

And beyond the car industry, we find technology striving for minification. The iPod is a small portable digital audio player designed and marketed by Apple Computer. And even though it's already a small product, Apple continues to release smaller and smaller versions of the popular iPod with larger and larger hard drives (thinking minification and magnification !)

Clothing designers are thinking small, too. There are entrepreneurs who specialize in baby clothes and small dog clothes, such as the Baby Ultimate Child Clothing and Baby Clothes Boutique *(www.babyultimate.com)* and the Pure Country Pet Boutique *(www.purecountry.net)*

Think rearrangement

Turn things around, backward, upside down or inside out. James Dyson, founder of Dyson vacuum cleaners, was tired of buying vacuums that lost suction as they filled up. Rather than improve on the existing designs, he started from scratch and rearranged the entire vacuum in a new and different, and ultimately highly successful, way. Dyson's new arrangement used cyclonic separation instead of a bag. Eight cylindrical cyclones whirl dirt and air at speeds up to 600 m.p.h. The machine uses centrifugal force to trap the dirt and expel the air. And, there is no filter to clog, which means the Dyson stays powerful. How successful has it been? In the past few years, he has sold over $10 billion worldwide. I'd say his rearrangement was a success!

How about turning something upside down? What's the problem with typical ketchup, mustard, and salad dressing bottles? It's hard to get the contents out, especially when the contents are running low. The solution? Manufacturers are now creating the bottles to stand upside down so the contents are always easy to get out.

What do you work with that can benefit from this kind of thinking? What can you turn around... revolutionize?

Rearrange things, change pace, alter sequence, start from scratch. This type of thinking works for everyone. For instance, salespeople can use these creative techniques to discover new applications for products or services, new ways to emphasize customer benefits, new ideas or product combinations to solve customer problems, better ways to organize their time and effort.

If you want to spur your mind to new action, think combination, adaptation, substitution, magnification, minification, and rearrangement. You'll be amazed with the ideas you'll develop. Before long, you'll be thinking in each of these ways as a matter of daily course. This kind of thinking increases the scope of your mind power and enables you to achieve fuller use of your mental capabilities. Let your mind work for you. Take nothing for granted. Everything can be changed, improved. The only thing you can count on for certain is change. Don't wait for it - be an agent of change. Help bring change about.

Chapter 7

The Devil's Wedge

HATRED, FEAR, OR JEALOUSY MAY LEAD A PERSON TO ACT UNWISELY, TO FIGHT OR RUN, BUT AT LEAST HE ACTS. THE WEDGE OF DISCOURAGEMENT DOES FAR MORE HARM - IT CAUSES YOU TO SIT DOWN, PITY YOURSELF, AND DO NOTHING.

Are you familiar with the old fable about the devil's sale? It's interesting. And like most old fables, it has a moral that's worth thinking about. The story goes that Satan was having a sale of his wares. There on display and offered for sale were the rapier of jealousy, the dagger of fear, and the strangling noose of hatred, each with its own high price. But standing alone on a purple pedestal, gleaming in the light was a worn and battered wedge. This was the devil's most prized possession. For with it alone, he could stay in business, and this was not for sale. It was the wedge of discouragement.

The devil prizes the wedge of discouragement above all else because of its enfeebling, demoralizing effect. Hatred, fear, or jealousy may lead an immature person to act unwisely, to fight or run or grab, but at least he acts. Discouragement, on the other hand, harms more than any of these - it causes you to sit down, pity yourself, and *do nothing.*

This doesn't have to happen, but unfortunately it all too frequently does. Not until we realize that discouragement is often a form of self-pity do we begin to take stock of ourselves and our predicament and decide to act, to do something that would take us out of an unpleasant situation. The answer to discouragement, to self-pity, then, is intelligent action.

The billionaire and founder of Combined Insurance Company, W. Clement Stone, formed the habit in the early days of his career of saying, "That's good!" whenever anything happened, good or bad. Most of the time, of course, it was something good. But even when he learned of a near calamity, a deadly serious situation that would have sent a lesser man scurrying for cover, he smiled and said, "That's good." Then as his associates shook their heads in resigned disbelief, he'd tear headlong into the problem and find what was good in it. Invariably, some elements in the situation could be turned to advantage, and he would find them and, more importantly, act on them.

Everyone has days or even successions of days when nothing seems to go right. Yet if we understand that something good can usually be grounded in almost any situation, we'll go quietly, efficiently to work on the most important part of the problem, the one that can be turned to advantage. Self-pity or inactivity cannot possibly help the situation. The only rational course to follow is to re-evaluate and move forward.

Some of the most successful have at one time or another been forced by a stretch of poor productivity to analyze their methods and use of time. Now a dry spell is no fun for anyone, but it's often the only situation extreme enough to get us to look at ourselves - to find out that what we're doing, why we're doing it, and what it is - is the best possible way it can be done. As Emerson said, "When a man is pushed, tormented, defeated... he has a chance to learn something."

Here's something else to think about: Discouragement very often comes on the heels of crisis. And it's been said that crises are thoroughfares; we can go either way, up or down. We go up out of a crisis by doing something constructive; we go down by wallowing around in our problems and feeling sorry for ourselves. Discouragement, which comes to all of us sooner or later, is a test of nature. Those who refuse to yield to it, in time pass through discouragement to the smooth and sunlit seas beyond. And what once seemed to be a storm with such voracity that it blotted out the whole world is soon forgotten.

Whenever you face discouragement, try to keep in mind three vitally important points. First, discouragement is often a form of self-pity, an expensive emotion we can get along very well without. And the most effective antidote for self-pity is intelligent action. Next, within any discouraging situation, there's almost always lurking an opportunity for growth, maturity, and future success. There's something good about it. And, finally, discouragement should be kept in its proper perspective. What may at the moment seem like the end of the world won't seem so important in 10 days or won't be very important in 10 months. Take the long-range view and you can't be defeated by momentary setbacks. The Chinese have a saying that if you live with a disaster for three years, it will turn into a blessing.

Being human qualifies us for some occasional pressure by the wedge of discouragement, but we have within us the strength to pull away and use it to our advantage. The next time you're tempted to feel discouraged about something, try taking the attitude of W. Clement Stone. Simply say, "That's good," and then start finding out what is good about it.

Chapter 8

The Profile of a Creative Person

CREATIVE PEOPLE, THOUGH THEY MAY BE DISSIMILAR IN MANY RESPECTS, SHARE AT THEIR CORE THREE FOUNDING CHARACTERISTICS NOT PRESENT IN PEOPLE OF AVERAGE ACHIEVEMENT.

REACH FOR IDEAS

The creative person realizes that his mind is an inexhaustible storehouse. It can provide anything he earnestly wants in life. But in order to draw from this storehouse, he must constantly augment its stock of information, thoughts, and wisdom. He reaches out for ideas. He respects the mind of others - gives credit to their mental abilities. Everyone has ideas - they're free - and many of them are excellent. By first listening to ideas and then thinking them through before judging them, the creative person avoids prejudice and close-mindedness. This is the way he maintains a creative "climate" around himself.

Ideas are like slippery fish. They seem to have a peculiar knack of getting away from us. Because of this, the creative person always has a pad and a pencil handy. When he gets an idea, he writes it down. He knows that many people have found their whole lives changed by a single great thought. By capturing ideas immediately, he doesn't risk forgetting them. *[Note: a great way to save ideas easily is to Text-Message them from your cell phone to your main email account. You are rarely without your cell phone, and this allows you to record your idea for later review and action.]*

Having a sincere interest in people, our creative person listens carefully when someone else is talking. He's intensely observant, absorbing everything he sees and hears. He behaves as if everyone he meets wears a sign that reads, "My ideas and interest may offer the hidden key to your next success." Thus, he makes it a point always to talk with other people's interest in mind. And it pays off in a flood of new ideas and information that would otherwise be lost to him forever.

Widening his circle of friends and broadening his base of knowledge are two more very effective techniques of the creative person.

ANTICIPATE ACHIEVEMENT

The creative person anticipates achievement. She expects to win. And the above-average production engendered by this kind of attitude affects those around her in a positive way. She's a plus-factor for all who know her.

Problems are challenges to creative minds. Without problems, there would be little reason to think at all. She knows it's a waste of time merely to worry about problems, so she wisely invests the same time and energy in solving problems.

When the creative person gets an idea, she puts it through a series of steps designed to improve it. She thinks in new directions. She builds big ideas from little ones and new ideas from old ones: associating ideas, combining them, adapting, substituting, magnifying, minifying, rearranging and reversing ideas.

BE CREATIVE FOR YOURSELF

Creative and productive people are not creative and productive for the benefit of others. It's because they're driven by the need to be creative and productive. They'd be creative and productive if they lived on a deserted island with no one benefiting or even aware of what they were doing. They experience the joy of producing something. That others benefit from it is fine, but only secondary.

This is a story of the painters who were before their time. Renoir was laughed at and rejected not only by the public but by his own fellow artists, yet he went right on painting. Even Manet said to Monet, "Renoir has no talent at all. You who are his friend should tell him kindly to give up painting."

A group of artists who were rejected by the establishment of their time formed their own association in self-defense. Do you know who was in that group? They were Degas, Pissaro, Monet, Cezanne, and Renoir. Five of the greatest artists of all time, all doing what they believed in, in the face of total rejection.

Renoir, in his later life, suffered terribly from rheumatism, especially in his hands. He lived in constant pain. And when Matisse visited the aging painter, he saw that every stroke was causing renewed pain, and he asked, "Why do you still have to work? Why continue to torture yourself?" And then Renoir answered, "The pain passes, but the pleasure, the creation of beauty, remains." One day when he was 78, finally quite famous and successful, he remarked, "I'm still making progress." The next day he died.

This is the mark of the creative person... still making progress, still learning, still producing as long as he or she lives, despite pain or problems of all kinds. Not producing for the joy or satisfaction of others, but because he must. Because it brings pleasure and satisfaction.

Chapter 9

A Commitment to Laughter

THE ONE SERIOUS CONVICTION THAT A MAN SHOULD HAVE IS THAT NOTHING IS TO BE TAKEN SERIOUSLY.

One of the enriching blessings of growing older all the time is that it has a way of improving one's sense of humor - or at least it should. The person without a good sense of humor is a person to avoid as though he were a known carrier of the plague.

Horace Walpole once said, "I have never yet seen or heard anything serious that was not ridiculous." And Samuel Butler said, "The one serious conviction that a man should have is that nothing is to be taken seriously." It has been said that seriousness is the only refuge of the shallow. Oscar Wilde said, "It is a curious fact that the worst work is always done with the best intentions, and that people are never so trivial as when they take themselves very seriously."

I remember that when I was in the service, one of the toughest jobs I had was to keep from laughing at the wrong times - during an admiral's inspection, for example. There is nothing funnier than the seriousness of the military, especially high-ranking military. The fancy costumes, the panoply, the shining sabers, the serious faces - it was all, to me, hilariously funny.

We can be serious about situations. When a youngster is ill or hurt, or someone insults your spouse, you can get very serious about the situation in a hurry. But that's not taking ourselves seriously. That's different.

The thing that bothered me about Hemingway, as much as I admired his work, was that I thought he tended to take himself too seriously. He didn't seem to be able to laugh at himself. And I think he suffered from this flaw in his character.

I have found it a good rule of thumb to be slightly suspicious of anyone who takes himself too seriously. There's usually something fishy there someplace. I think this is why we love children so much: Life is a game to them. They will do their best at whatever work is given them, but they never seem to lose their ebullient sense of humor; there is always a sparkle of humor in their eyes. When a child lacks this, he is usually in need of help.

Dictators are famous for their lack of humor. The mark of a cruel person is that he doesn't seem to be able to see anything funny in the world. And, a sense of humor was what was so great about Mark Twain. No matter how serious the subject, he could find the humor in it and bring it out. All the great comedians have this ability to see what's funny in the so-called serious situation. They can poke fun at themselves. There are those who believe that a sense of humor is the only thing that has kept the human race from totally extinguishing itself.

People who are emotionally healthy, with a sense of proportion, are cheerful people. They tend to look upon the bright side of things and see a lot of humor in their daily lives. They're not Pollyannas - they know what's going on and that a lot of it's not at all funny - but they don't permit the dark side of things to dominate their lives. To my mind, when a person lacks a sense of humor, there's something pretty seriously wrong with him.

Samuel Butler said,

"A sense of humor keen enough to show a man his own absurdities as well as those of other people will keep a man from the commission of all sins, or nearly all, save those that are worth committing."

It took a sense of humor to write that, and only people with blank spaces where their senses of humor should be will find it offensive. There's something so healthy about laughter, especially when it's directed at ourselves.

There are times for all of us when all the laughter seems to be gone, but we should not permit these periods to last too long. When we've lost our sense of humor, there isn't very much left. We become ridiculous. We must then go to war against the whole world, and that's a war we cannot win.

Chapter 10

A Time to Risk or Sit

THERE IS A TIME WHEN WE MUST DECIDE EITHER
TO RISK EVERYTHING TO FULFILL OUR DREAMS OR
SIT FOR THE REST OF OUR LIVES IN THE BACKYARD.

In 1965, Robert M. Manry, a copy editor for the *Cleveland
Plain Dealer,* sailed from the United States to England in a 13-
foot sailboat - 3,200 miles across the North Atlantic in a boat
so small you'd hesitate to take it out on Lake Michigan or Long
Island Sound as small-craft warnings were flying.

For 78 days Manry and his tiny 36-year-old sailboat battled
one of the toughest stretches of saltwater on earth. Gales blew
the boat on its side. Manry tried to nap during the day and
sailed at night so that he could try to avoid being run down and
chopped into kindling and hamburger by great ocean-going
steamers. On several occasions, he was washed over the side in
heavy seas. Each time he would haul himself back aboard by a
lifeline he kept tied to himself in the boat. He suffered terrible
hallucinations, the result of having to take so many pep pills to
stay awake during the long nights.

Why? What made him do it? It wasn't publicity; he went about
the whole thing so quietly - practically no one knew what he
was up to. He thought no one would pay attention to him, and
that was fine with him.

The reason was that he had dreamed of sailing the Atlantic
ever since he had been a small boy. He bought the dinky old
boat for $250. He completely rebuilt her, taught himself
navigation, and practiced long-distance sailing on Lake Erie.

He told his wife the real reason for his embarking on so incredible a journey in so vulnerable a craft. He said to her, *"There is a time when one must decide either to risk everything to fulfill one's dreams or sit for the rest of one's life in the backyard."* Now this is why Mr. Manry went sailing over the mountains of deep water in a boat only about twice the size of your bathtub. This is why he sat in his tiny open cockpit and weathered storms that caused the passengers to clear the weather decks of giant ocean liners. He was fulfilling a dream he'd carried in his heart since he'd been a small boy.

As a result, offers for books and magazine articles poured in to him. Cleveland gave him a hero's welcome, as did the 20,000 people who wildly cheered the successful end of his voyage when he arrived in Falmouth, England. It's been proposed to Congress that Manry's boat, *Tinkerbelle,* be placed in the Smithsonian Institution alongside Charles Lindbergh's plane, *Spirit of St. Louis.*

But all this fame and sudden stature in the eyes of the world - this was not why he made the trip. It was because he believes that there is a time when one must decide either to risk everything to fulfill one's dreams or sit for the rest of one's life in the backyard.

Courage, the courage to finally take one's life in one's own hands and go after the big dream, has a way of making that dream come true. It seems to open hidden doorways from which good things begin to pour into one's life. But only after we've made the journey in our own way. For Manry, at 47 years of age, it was sailing 3,200 miles of the North Atlantic. Each of us must make his own voyage through darkness and danger to the light that beacons in the distance. A journey to fulfillment... or sit in the backyard.

Chapter 11

The Entrepreneurial Adventure

It takes longer than we realize, and the journey is an arduous one. But, one day we wake up, and we've achieved a kind of independence never known or perhaps understood by the employee, no matter how high he or she may travel in the hushed corridors of executive country.

All business activity in the United States and its territories began as entrepreneurial adventures. Trace any corporation back to its beginnings, or the beginnings of its parent corporation, or the beginning of its parent's corporation, as is sometimes the case, and you'll find it began as an idea that would fill or help fill a need or desire on the part of human beings who would become customers.

We look today at a complex multinational organization like IBM and forget that the company began in the mind of a single human being. Anyone who starts or causes to be started a business venture, is an entrepreneur.

The entrepreneurial adventure is endlessly attractive to those endowed with entrepreneurial spirits; adventurers, in varying degrees, whose visions of the future tend to be hopeful and enthusiastic, rather than defeatist.

The entrepreneur is the person who says, "I think it'll be a big success." The non-entrepreneur says, "You're going to lose your shirt."

A survey taken many years ago of the most successful people in a large American city turned up the fact that most of their ultimate success depended in large measure on the jobs they had lost; whether they had resigned or had been fired wasn't all that important. And under questioning, those very successful people thought about that interesting fact for perhaps the first time and shuddered to think of what their present lives might have been like had they clung to one of those early jobs which, at the time, seemed so important to them and their families.

Now they're not all entrepreneurs, of course, but they were people with faith in themselves and their ideas, which is the mark of success, wherever it's found. During those important steps in their careers, they were no doubt warned by well-meaning relatives and friends to hang on to that job they had held, and lectured on the dark and dismal pitfalls of venturing off on something as ephemeral and evanescent as an idea. But of course, good ideas are not as ephemeral or evanescent as their status in thought might indicate to the more fearful. They're the most important things on the planet earth, and it's producing ideas that raises the human being to his or her highest levels of achievement.

Ideas solve problems and make our lives infinitely more interesting and rewarding, less dangerous, better fed, better employed, richer in countless ways, and wonderfully more comfortable. Without ideas, we'd still be sitting in the trees grooming one another. All the creatures on the planet have life-saving techniques. Some are fleet of foot, others sharp of claw and fang. There are fish in the deep, dark trenches of the ocean that dangle tiny lanterns above their waiting jaws. But for the human being, there is the brain, the idea producer, to save his or her skin in a myriad of ways. And the United States, the first nation in history with the word *happiness* in its official chartering papers, offers a number of options to those desiring to share in the good life. One of those options is the right to go into business with little more than an idea and the determination to succeed.

The idea that results and a person running the risks of starting his or her own business depend strictly upon the person - regardless of background, education, previous level of accomplishment, and aspirations. For most of us, going into business is a pursuit beset by many problems, irritations, headaches, sleepless nights, long hours, and low pay. Ah, yes, being in business for one's self does not necessarily mean an inordinately high income. On the contrary, *it often means very little or no income at all for long periods of time. But once the business hits, whether it takes five years or 15, you've got the world by the nether parts.* You decide what you're worth in the salary and bonus departments. And the company can pay for much that would ordinarily come out of an employee's pay.

America's top executives working for large multinational corporations usually earn more in salary and perks, stock options, and bonuses than the great majority of entrepreneurs. But the entrepreneur has something else. He has control. And once the business is truly successful, which means it's probably in a state of happy expansion, he or she can hire the best executives to run things while he or she takes a few months' rest in Hawaii or Greece or plays golf in Nairobi and does a bit of deep-sea fishing in the Seychelles.

You say it might take 15 years for that kind of success? Yes, I do. But how long would it take you if you worked for IBM or Chrysler, 15 or 20 years I suppose, if ever, right? And the 15 years aren't all pain and suffering and sleepless nights. There's a lot of joy in there, too. There's the joy of seeing your own ideas in action and of watching your own ideas and efforts win against the competition. There's the joy of watching the money pour in along with the orders. There's a, sort of, kind vindication in that.

When I resigned from CBS, my friends told me repeatedly what an idiot I was. I had reached the top. I went to work in the beautifully paneled brass-trimmed elevators of the world-famous Wrigley Building in Chicago. I rubbed shoulders with the rich and famous, and I earned top dollar in my profession. Man, I was on top of the heap. I had it made, and I was only 28 years old. But I dreamed to be an entrepreneur - in total control of my destiny - and as my friends learned, it does little good to remonstrate with an entrepreneur.

Christopher Columbus, brilliant navigator that he was, could have spent his life in peace navigating up and down the coastal waters of Europe and remaining within the known boundaries of the period's world's maps. But at the edges of the known waters there appeared the terrifying legend: "Here there be dragons." And it was there that Columbus desired to sail. And it's there that every entrepreneur desires to sail.

It's interesting to note that on the maps beyond the known world, there was never a legend reading, *"Here there be unlimited opportunity for exploration, no doubt much gold and silver and precious gems, and strange creatures living beyond these boundaries waiting for discoveries and development for the daring and intrepid sailor. "* Even though it had always been that way before, no one ever suggested that it might also be that way in still undiscovered areas. It's the natural proclivity of cartographers and advice givers to look upon the unknown as bad. For they, like children going into a darkened basement alone, feel that the dark and the unknown must hold strange and fearful creatures unimaginable in the known and lighted world.

They cannot think otherwise. It's their nature. Yet, at the time of Columbus, not a single live dragon had ever been seen upon the planet earth by anyone. Dragons were, in fact, fairytale creatures, yet they always inhabited the uncharted regions of the world. It said so right on the maps.

So when you get an idea that you think will result in an excellent business of your own - and it needn't be a new idea by any means - keep it to yourself and your secret notepad for a period of time while you simmer it on the rotisserie of your mind's consciousness and unconsciousness. Let it turn while you view it from every angle. Look at it from the standpoint of the worst possible scenario. If it's a good, sound idea, it should survive even the worst times, as good businesses do.

It usually takes longer than we realize when we begin. At the decision to become an entrepreneur, we seldom take into consideration the length and arduous nature of the contract. But if our idea is sound, and if we are sound, and if we fully understand the concept of service and the importance of working capital and constant upgrading of our product or service, and if we have the perseverance of Columbus, we'll wake up some fine morning to find ourselves one of the competent ones of our generation. We've achieved a kind of independence never known or perhaps understood by the employee, no matter how high he or she may travel in the hushed corridors of executive country.

Chapter 12

The Cure for Procrastination

WHAT OVERWHELMS US IS NOT THE WORK ITSELF. IT'S THINKING HOW HARD IT'S GOING TO BE. IT'S SEEING IT GET LARGER EVERY DAY. IT'S PUTTING IT OFF AND HOPING THAT SOMEHOW, THROUGH SOME MIRACLE, IT WILL DISAPPEAR.

Have you ever noticed that the longer you look at something you should be doing, the more difficult it seems to appear? That the longer you put off something you should do, the more difficult it is to get started?

A good deal of frustration and unhappiness could be avoided if people would just do what they know they should do.

The great newspaper editor Arthur Brisbane once wrote, "Don't exaggerate your own importance, your own size, or your own miseries. You are an ant in a human anthill. Be a working ant - not a ridiculous insect pitying yourself." Strong language, maybe, but there's a lot of sense in it.

A person carrying a heavy weight is all right as long as he keeps moving. The minute he stops, puts the weight on the ground, and sits down to rest, the weight seems to become heavier; the distance to be traveled, greater; and the work, just that much more unpleasant.

Sometimes it must seem to everyone that things have piled up so high that there's just no way of digging out. But there is. Pick the thing that's most important to do, and simply begin doing it. Just by digging in, you'll feel better, and you'll find that it's not nearly as bad as you thought it would be. Keep at it, and before long, that pile of things to do that seemed so overwhelming is behind you - finished.

What overwhelms us is not the work itself. It's thinking how hard it's going to be. It's seeing it get larger every day. It's putting if off and hoping that somehow, through some miracle, it will disappear.

The Chinese have a saying that a journey of a thousand miles begins with but a single step. And that step accomplishes two things. First, it automatically shortens the distance we still have to travel, and, second, and just as important, it makes us feel better, more hopeful - it strengthens our faith. If a person will just keep putting one foot in front of the other, he will be taken into new and exciting places, see new and interesting things, and think thoughts that never would have come to him if he'd remained at the starting point. Then the journey is finished. He wonders how or why he could ever have sat so long and worried and stewed about the time and trouble it would involve to do what he knew he should do.

If you'll think back, you'll remember that you've always been happiest, most contented, after having finished a difficult project or faced up to a responsibility you were worried about. It's never as bad as you think it's going to be, and the joy that will come with its accomplishment makes it more than worthwhile.

Work never killed anyone. It's worry that does the damage. And the worry would disappear if we'd just settle down and do the work.

As Calvin Coolidge put it, "All growth depends upon activity. There is no development physically or intellectually without effort, and effort means work. Work is not a curse; it is the prerogative of intelligence, the only means to manhood, and the measure of civilization. "

Chapter 13

The Great Problem-Solving Tool

Successful people are not without problems. They're simply people who've learned to solve their problems.

All creatures on earth are supplied at birth with everything they need for successful survival. All creatures except one are supplied with a set of instincts that will do the job for them. And because of that, most creatures don't need much of a brain. In the Pulitzer Prize-winning playwright Archibald MacLeish's play *The Secret of Freedom,* a character says, *"The only thing about a man that is man is his mind. Everything else you can find in a horse. "* That's uncomfortably true.

Take the magnificent bald eagle for example. To see one of them swooping down and pluck a live and sizeable fish from the water on a single pass is astonishing. More astonishing still is the eagle's eyesight. And because of its need to see small rodents moving in the grass from high altitudes or a fish just inches under the surface of the water, its incredible eyes take up just about all the space in its head. For the eagle, its eyes are the most important thing, and everything else works in unison with them. Its brain is tiny and rudimentary. It doesn't think or plan or remember; it simply acts in accordance with stimuli.

And it's the same with most other living creatures. Even the beautiful porpoise, with a much larger brain, and the chimpanzee are easily tamed and taught. Only one takes 20 years to mature and has dominion over all the rest on the earth itself, and has today the power to destroy all life on earth in a couple of hours. Only one is given the godlike power to fashion its own life according to the images it holds in its remarkable mind.

The human mind is the one thing that separates us from the rest of the creatures on earth. Everything that means anything to us comes to us through our minds, our love of our families, our beliefs, all of our talents, knowledge, abilities. Everything is reflected through our minds. Anything that comes to us in the future will almost certainly come to us as a result of the extent to which we use our minds.

And yet, it's the last place on earth the average person will turn to for help. You know why? You know why people don't automatically turn their own vast mental resources on when faced with a problem? It's because they never learned *how* to think. Most people will go to any length to avoid thinking when they're faced with a problem. They will ask advice from the most illogical people, usually people who don't know any more than they do: next-door neighbors, members of their families, and friends stuck in the same mental traps that they are. Very few of them use the muscles of their mind to solve their problems.

Yet living successfully, getting the things we want from life, is a matter of solving the problems that stand between where we are now and the point we wish to reach. No one is without problems. They're part of living. But let me show you how much time we waste in worrying about the wrong problems. Here's a reliable estimate of the things people worry about: Things that never happen: 40%. Things over and past that can never be changed by all the worry in the world: 30%. Needless worries about our health: 12%. Petty miscellaneous worries: 10%. Real legitimate worries: 8%.

In short, 92% of the average person's worries take up valuable time, cause painful stress, even mental anguish, and are absolutely unnecessary. And of the real legitimate worries, there are two kinds. There are the problems we can solve, and there are the problems beyond our ability to personally solve. But most of our real problems usually fall into the first group, the ones we can solve, if we'll learn how.

The average working person has at his or her disposal an enormous amount of free time. In fact, you'll see if you'll total the hours in a year and subtract the sleeping hours: If we sleep 8 hours every night, we have about 6,000 waking hours, of which less than 2,000 are spent on the job. Now this leaves 4,000 hours a year when a person is neither working nor sleeping. These can be called discretionary hours with which that person can do pretty much as he or she pleases.

So that you can see the amazing results in your own life, I want to recommend that you take just one hour a day, five days a week, and devote this hour to exercising your mind. You don't even have to do it on weekends. Pick one hour a day on which you can fairly regularly count. The best time for me is an hour before the others are up in the morning. The mind's clear, the house is quiet, and, if you like, with a fresh cup of coffee, this is the time to start the mind going.

During this hour every day take a completely blank sheet of paper. At the top of the page write your present primary goal clearly, simply. Then, since our future depends on the way in which we handle our work, write down as many ideas as you can for improving that which you now do. Try to think of 20 possible ways in which the activity that fills your day can be improved. You won't always get 20, but even one idea is good.

Now remember two important points with regard to this. One, this is not particularly easy, and, two, most of your ideas won't be any good. When I say it's not easy, I mean it's like starting any new habit. At first you'll find your mind a little reluctant to be hauled up out of that old familiar bed. But as you think about your work and ways in which it might be improved, write down every idea that pops into your head, no matter how absurd it might seem.

The most important thing that this extra hour accomplishes is that it deeply embeds your goal into your subconscious mind, starts the whole vital machine reworking the first thing every morning. And 20 ideas a day, if you can come up with that many, total 100 a week, even skipping weekends. An hour a day, five days a week, totals 260 hours a year and still leaves you 3,740 hours of free leisure time. Now this means you'll be thinking about your goal and ways of improving your performance, increasing your service six full extra working weeks a year, 6,112 40-hour weeks devoted to thinking and planning. Can you see how easy it is to rise above that so-called competition? And it'll still leave you with seven hours a day to spend as you please.

Starting each day thinking, and you'll find that your mind will continue to work all day long. And you'll find that at odd moments, when you least expect it, really great ideas will begin to bubble up from your subconscious. When they do, write them down as soon as you can. Just one great idea can completely revolutionize your work and, as a result, your life.

Each time you write your goal at the top of the sheet of paper, don't worry or become concerned about it. Think of it as only waiting to be reached, a problem only waiting to be solved. Face it with faith and bend all the great powers of your mind toward solving it. And believe me, solve it you will. This puts each of us in the driver's seat.

Each of us has a tendency to underestimate his or her own abilities. We should realize that we have deep within ourselves deep reservoirs of great ability, even genius that can be tapped if we'll just dig deep enough. It's the miracle of your mind.

Everything fashioned by human beings is a result of goal setting. We reach our goals. That's how we know that the diseases that plague us will be conquered. We've set goals to eradicate every disease that plagues us and eradicate them we will, one by one. We have never set a goal that we have not reached or are now in the process of reaching.

Chapter 14

Is Your Personal Corporation Growing?

ALL RESPONSIBLE COMPANY OFFICERS KNOW THAT UNLESS THE COMPANY IS GROWING, IT'S DEVELOPING THE FIRST SIGNS OF DEATH. THE SAME LAW APPLIES TO YOU.

Every person is, in reality, in business for himself or herself in that each is building his or her own life regardless of who happens to write his or her paycheck. So for the purpose of this message, think of yourself as a corporation. You hold the office of president of this corporation, and you're responsible for its success or failure. You and the members of your family are stockholders in your corporation, and it's your responsibility to see that the value of the stock increases in the years ahead.

If your company is growing, it will have a tendency to continue to grow. In other words, you're doing things right. Conversely, a company that is going backwards or shrinking has a tendency to continue to go backwards or shrink until acted upon by an outside force. All responsible company officers know that unless the company is growing, it's developing the first signs of death. As the head of your personal corporation, you must realize that this same law applies to you as well.

However, a person has a tremendous advantage over even the largest corporation. Think of any large multinational corporation. Can it double its production in a single day? Of course not. Can it double its sales in a single day? Of course not. It would like to, but its growth must be gradual and steady because of the interconnecting complexities of operating such a large organization. *Yet a person can double, triple, quadruple his or her effectiveness in a month or less.* It's like comparing the movement of a single scout to the movement of a great army.

Can you grow and improve as a person at least 10% a year? Of course you can. In fact, experts estimate a person can increase his or her effectiveness anywhere from 50% to 100% and more within 30 days.

History is filled with people who exceeded their previous performance to an almost unbelievable extent. People in management and in production who multiplied their effectiveness many times. Students who moved from failing grades to straight A's and the Dean's List. People in sales who found they could, through the proper management of their abilities, minds, and time, sell as much of their company's products in a single month as they had previously sold in an entire year. Think about what that means.

If you waste even an hour of productive time every workday, it adds up to 250 hours a year. That time wasted could shut your corporation down! You can earn nothing with the doors closed. What is your time worth an hour? Multiply this by 250 and you can see what you're throwing away. Now whether your employer pays for this wasted hour or not is unimportant. Life will not pay for it.

How much are you worth right now, today, as a corporation? What's your value today, to yourself, your family, your company? If you were an outside investor, a stranger, would you invest in this corporation? A company growing at the rate of 10% a year will double in size in about eight years. What attention are you giving to the growth of your personal corporation?

Chapter 15

Falling Isn't Failing

MANY PEOPLE NEVER ACHIEVE SUCCESS BECAUSE THEY EQUATE FALLING TO FAILING. HOWEVER, FALLING ISN'T FAILING UNLESS YOU DON'T GET BACK UP.

Mary Pickford used to say, "Don't look at the sudden loss of a habit, or a way of life, as the end of the road; see it instead as only a bend in the road that will open up all sorts of interesting possibilities and new experiences. After all, you've seen the scenery on the old road for so long, and you obviously no longer like it."

The breaking of a long-time habit does seem like the end of the road at the time - the complete cessation of enjoyment. Suddenly dropping the habit so fills our minds with the desire for the old habitual way that, for a while, it seems there will no longer be any peace, any sort of enjoyment. But that's not true. New habits form in a surprisingly short time, and a whole new world opens up to us.

For those who have tried repeatedly to break a habit of some kind, only to repeatedly fail, Mary Pickford said, *"Falling is not failing, unless you fail to get up." Most people who finally win the battle over a habit have done so only after repeated failures.*

I remember in Arthur Miller's play *The Price,* the father lost everything during the stock market crash of 1929 and, for the rest of his life, sat in a room in the attic of a relative. That's failing. It seems some people lack the stamina, the energy, to do it all over again or to make a new start. For them, it's just the end of the road, and they've come to a full stop. Many lead such superficial lives, have so little depth of mind and spirit that the sudden loss of income or material things is too much for them, and they jump out a window or retreat into insanity.

So if you've been trying to start in a new direction, you might do well to remember the advice of Mary Pickford: It isn't the end of the road; it's just a bend in the road. And falling isn't failing, unless you don't get up.

Chapter 16

The $25,000 Idea

A successful life is built on the foundation of successful tasks - each completed in the pursuit of perfection - one day at a time.

A goal sometimes seems so far off and our progress often appears to be so painfully slow that we have a tendency to lose heart. It sometimes seems we'll never make the grade. We come close to giving up - falling back into old habits, which, while they may be comfortable, lead to nowhere. Well, there's a way to overcome this inevitable barrier to success, and here is the secret: Every great achievement is nothing more than the collection of smaller achievements done to perfection. Even the "impossible" has been accomplished through the relentless pursuit of success, one day at a time.

Have you ever seen a bricklayer starting a new building by putting the first brick in place? You are struck by the size of the job he has ahead of him. But one day, almost before you realize it, he's finished. All the thousands of bricks are in place, each one vital to the finished structure, each one sharing its portion of the load. How did he do it? Simple: one brick at a time. And so is the pursuit of success and greatness.

A lifetime is composed of days, strung together into weeks, months, and years. A successful life is nothing more than a lot of successful days put together. As such, every day counts.

Just as a stonemason can put only one stone in place at a time, you can live only one day at a time. And it's the way in which these stones are placed that will determine the beauty, the strength of the tower. If each stone is successfully placed - with care and quality - the tower will be a success. If, on the other hand, they're put down in a hit-or-miss fashion - irrespective of quality - the whole tower is in danger. Seems simple. Yet, how many people do you know who live like this - focused on "just getting through" each day instead of on the "success" of each day. Which are you focused on?

The Habit of Success

Do each day all that can be done that day. You don't need to overwork or to rush blindly into your work trying to do the greatest possible number of things in the shortest possible time. Don't try to do tomorrow's or next week's work today. It's not the number of things you do, but the quality, the efficiency of each separate action that count.

To achieve this "habit of success," you need only to focus on the most important tasks and succeed in each small task of each day. Enough of these and you have a successful week, month, year, and lifetime. Success is not a matter of luck. It can be predicted and guaranteed, and anyone can achieve it by following this plan.

But most people live a life of quiet mediocrity and never achieve the success they truly desire because they get impatient. They want easy success or none at all. They see the path to success as a frustration, an impediment. Each day spent short of the ultimate goal is viewed as a time of failure and as an annoyance. As such, they get distracted by hundreds of little things that each day try to get us off our course. Yet the successful among us know the truth: If the end goal is all we desire, we simply cannot put in the time and effort it takes to be a success when it counts - each day - and therefore cannot lay the foundation for tomorrow's success.

Pay no attention to petty distractions. Enjoy the easy days and shake off the bad days. Stay steadily on your track. Concentrate on each task of the day from morning to night and do each as successfully as you can. Know full well that if each of your tasks is performed successfully, or at least the greater majority of them, your life *must* be successful.

The $25,000 Idea

Now how do we separate the important tasks from the unimportant? Did you ever hear of the single idea for which a man was paid $25,000? And it was worth every penny of it. The story goes that the president of a big steel company had granted an interview to an efficiency expert named Ivy Lee. Lee was telling his prospective client how he could help him do a better job of managing the company, when the president broke in to say something to the effect that he wasn't at present managing as well as he knew how. He went on to tell Ivy Lee that what was needed wasn't more knowing but a lot more doing. He said, "We know what we should be doing. Now if you can show us a better way of getting it done, I'll listen to you and pay you anything within reason you ask."

Well, Lee then said that he could give him something in 20 minutes that would increase his efficiency by at least 50 percent. He then handed the executive a blank sheet of paper and said, "Write down on this paper the six most important things you have to do tomorrow." Well, the executive thought about it and did as requested. It took him about three or four minutes.

Then Lee said, "Now number those items in the order of their importance to you or to the company." Well, that took another three or four or five minutes, and then Lee said, "Now put the paper in your pocket. And the first thing tomorrow morning, take it out and look at item number one. Don't look at the others, just number one, and start working on it. And if you can, stay with it until it's completed. Then take item number two the same way, then number three, and so on, till you have to quit for the day.

"Don't worry if you've only finished one or two; the others can wait. If you can't finish them all by this method, you could not have finished them with any other method. And without some system, you'd probably take 10 times as long to finish them and might not even have them in the order of their importance.

"Do this every working day," Lee went on. "After you've convinced yourself of the value of this system, have your people try it. Try it as long as you like. And then send me your check for whatever you think the idea is worth."

The entire interview hadn't taken more than a half-hour. In a few weeks the story has it that the company president sent Ivy Lee a check for $25,000 with a letter saying the lesson was the most profitable, from a money standpoint, he'd ever learned in his life. And it was later said that in five years this was the plan that was largely responsible for turning what was then a little-known steel company into one of the biggest independent steel producers in the world. One idea: the idea of taking things one at a time in their proper order. Of staying with one task until it's successfully completed before going on to the next.

For the next seven days try the $25,000 idea in your life. Tonight write down the six most important things you have to do. Then number them in the order of their importance. And tomorrow morning, go to work on number one. Stay with it till it's successfully completed, then move on to number two, and so on. When you've finished with all six, get another piece of paper and repeat the process. You'll be astonished and delighted at the order it brings into your life and at the rate of speed with which you'll be able to accomplish the things that need doing in the order of their importance. This simple but tremendously effective method will take all the confusion out of your life. You'll never find yourself running around in circles wondering what to do next.

The reason for writing down what you consider only the most important things to do is obvious. Handling each task during the day successfully is important to the degree of the importance of the tasks themselves. Doing a lot of unnecessary things successfully can be pretty much of a waste of time. Make certain that the tasks you take the time to do efficiently are important tasks, tasks that move you ahead steadily toward your goal.

Remember that you need not worry about tomorrow or the next day or what's going to happen at the end of the month. One day at a time, handled successfully, will carry you over every hurdle. It will solve every problem. You can relax in the happy knowledge that successful tasks make successful days, which in turn build a successful life. This is the kind of unassailable logic no one can argue with. It will work every time for every person.

Chapter 1 7

The Fog of Worry

(Only 8% of Worries are Worth It)

According to the Bureau of Standards, "A dense fog covering seven city blocks, to a depth of 100 feet, is composed of something less than one glass of water." So, if all the fog covering seven city blocks, 100 feet deep, were collected and held in a single drinking glass, it would not even fill it. And this could be compared to our worries. If we can see into the future and if we could see our problems in their true light, they wouldn't tend to blind us to the world, to living itself, but instead could be relegated to their true size and place. And if all the things most people worry about were reduced to their true size, you could probably put them all into a drinking glass, too.

It's a well-established fact that as we get older, we worry less. With the passing of the years and the problems each of them yields, we learn that most of our worries are not really worth bothering ourselves about too much and that we can manage to solve the important ones.

But to younger people, they often find their lives obscured by the fog of worry. Yet, here's an authoritative estimate of what most people worry about.

1. Things that never happen: 40 percent. That is, 40 percent of the things you worry about will never occur anyway.

2. Things over and past that can't be changed by all the worry in the world: 30 percent.

3. Needless worries about our health: 12 percent.

4. Petty, miscellaneous worries: 10 percent.

5. Real, legitimate worries: 8 percent.
   Only 8 percent of your worries are worth concerning yourself about. Ninety-two percent are pure fog with no substance at all.

Chapter 18

The Boss

You have only one boss and every person from the president of the largest corporation to the shoeshine boy has the same - he is simply the customer.

I want to tell you a little story that could make a wonderful difference in your life. You may already know about everything I'm going to tell you. If you do, you're a remarkable person, and according to the latest statistics you belong to the top 5% of all the working people in the world. You're to be congratulated. If you don't know about the things I'm going to say, you've been holding yourself back, not only on the job but you're also missing a big percentage of the greatest joy in life. I want to talk about your boss and your relationship with him. How you handle this relationship will determine your success or failure. It will determine how much money you make or do not make, and it will determine whether you're a happy person or an unhappy person.

So let's talk about you and your boss. Who is your boss? You have only one and every working person, from the president of the largest corporation to the shoeshine boy, has the same boss. He is simply *the customer*. There never has been, there is not now, and there never will be any boss but the customer. He is the one boss you must please. Everything you own he has paid for. He buys your home, your cars, your clothes. He pays for your vacations and puts your children through school. He pays your doctor bills and writes every paycheck you will ever receive. He will give you every promotion you will ever obtain during your lifetime, and he will discharge you if you displease him.

Sometimes, particularly these days of seemingly complex economics and big business, we lose sight of just what business is. It all started back during the most primitive times. A man, in order to fend for himself and his family, had to provide his own food and his own shelter. He had to do his own fighting and fashion his own rough clothes and crude weapons for hunting and materials for fishing. Later he had to manufacture his own farming implements. In short, each person had to personally take care of every department of his or her life.

Naturally it came about that men and women with certain talents appeared. One person was particularly adept at fashioning spears, another at fishing, another at hunting, another at making garments, and so on. It was only natural that soon these individuals found that they could best spend most of their time in the pursuit of that at which they were most talented and trade their production for the production of others.

As a result, the person who made spears found that others would give him a share of their food, clothing, and so on, if he'd provide them with spears. Thus, trade and commerce began. It's far more complex today but still based on the same principle. A person's money is the result of his production, and he trades it for things he needs and wants. And it's here that logical discrimination comes into the picture.

Since his money is the result of his work, it's left to his discretion as to where he spends it. It is here that he assumes the role of boss. He will spend his money only with those whom he feels have earned it. And this is as it should be. You and I are exactly the same way. If someone treats you badly in any way, you instinctively feel that he has not earned your business and you will withhold it from him.

Over a period of time this amounts to a really substantial penalty. Let's say a family spends $100 a week for food, and because they've been mistreated or even get the feeling they're not appreciated or liked, they stop doing business at one store and take their business to another one. That's a penalty to one store of $5,200 a year and an increase of that amount at another store. In 10 years it amounts to $52,000. This amount of money can be lost by not realizing who the boss really is. The same thing applies to our clothes, drug items, hardware, cleaning, gasoline, automobiles, everything we purchase.

The average family earns more than $42,000 a year. This money pays your salary and mine if we earn it. And our prosperity as individuals hinges directly on our attitude toward what we do for a living. The man who works on an automotive assembly line might not think much about the car at the point of sale, nor about the family who will eventually buy and travel in that car. But that family pays his salary, and they will withhold the purchase of the car on which he works if it does not earn their respect and admiration.

If you doubt this even for a moment, think of the cars that once were popular and that can no longer be seen on the road. This applies to all products. Having earned a successful place in the economy should not be confused with keeping it. It must be earned every day, year in, year out. There's not a single company that could not go out of business. Everything depends on how the boss is treated, the boss being the customer. And yet the customer is eminently fair, just as you are. He can be won back, and if he's treated with the importance that he deserves, he can in a few years bring a lot of other people into your place of business.

Let me tell you something you may not have thought about. If you get in your car and start driving across the country, you will pass many thousands of businesses, from small restaurants, drug stores, grocery stores, gas stations, to great sprawling corporate complexes covering hundreds of acres and employing thousands of people. By simply looking at each one you can tell how they're treating the boss.

Did you know that your rewards are in exact proportion to your service? That's right. We're paid exactly what we earn, but no more. And you can tell by looking at any business exactly what it has earned by seeing what it has. It's the same with people.

We get back exactly what we earn, but not a penny more. And this, again, is just the way it should be. A person might be underpaid for a while, but the scales of life must balance eventually and he will, in the end, receive just what he's earned.

There are of course two ways in which we're paid for what we do. One is tangible in the form of money, and the other is intangible, but just as important. To many it's more important. This latter form of payment comes in the form of inner satisfaction, in the form of joy as a result of accomplishment. It also comes in the form of satisfaction in position and the standing it gives us.

So each of us is paid in these two ways: money and satisfaction. And there's a very simple way to increase both of these forms of income. You may wonder how I can say that I can tell you of a simple way to increase your income from the standpoint of money as well as inner satisfaction. Yet I can, and you'll be able to see and spend the results.

First, I want you to understand and believe completely the great law that lies as the foundation of all life, business and personal. It is that our rewards in life will be in exact proportion to our service. The more you think about this and observe people and businesses in their true light, the more you'll see the undeniable truth of it.

Try as best you can to estimate the proportion of your total ability you have been giving to your work. I don't think anyone gives 100%. I don't think it's possible to give 100% day in and day out. But estimate what you consider to be the percentage of 100% you have been giving to your work. Would you say it's been 30%? 50%?

Since your rewards will be in exact proportion to your service, you can increase your income both financially and from an inner satisfaction standpoint simply by narrowing the distance between what you have been giving to your work and the 100% of which it may be said you could give under ideal conditions. You don't have to ask for a raise; the income will appear of its own accord and in the right time. You may want to question this, but try to take my word for it.

The second point I want to make is this: If you will begin to do your work better, better than you've ever done before, you will immediately begin to receive incalculably more inner satisfaction. You'll also find that what may have been a boring or uninteresting job will take on new meaning and interest. No matter what it is that you do during the entire working day, try in every case to do a little more than you have to, more than you're being paid for. Because unless you do more than you're being paid for now, you can't hope for or justify an increase in pay.

The third point is, each of us is interdependent. As I pointed out earlier, other people pay our salaries, buy our homes, clothe, feed, and educate our children. Therefore we depend on others for our very lives, just as they must depend on us. If we expect others to give us excellent service and fine products for the money we spend, doesn't it make good sense that we should treat them the same way? Every hour spent at our work should be spent in the attempt to give the best of which we are capable, a baker's dozen for the money our company's customers spend for our products and services and with which our salaries are paid.

A person who tries to get the maximum return for the minimum of effort is only kidding himself. Sooner or later the scales will balance. They must, for that is the law whether we like it or not. This kind of individual actually shrinks as a person, as a human being. He has no real place in a dynamic and swiftly changing world.

The fourth point is to try each day to find some way in which the work you're doing can be improved. Here again you're guaranteeing an increase in your income in both categories. We all know the cynical type of individual who will laugh at this. I know them; you know them. But I don't know one who could be said to be doing well, do you?

I know lots of men and women at the top of their fields who live their lives every day in the way I have suggested. Rather than go along with someone who's never proved in his own life that he knows what he's talking about, I'd prefer to believe the one who said, "As ye sow, so shall ye reap." I feel, as I'm sure you do, that he was more qualified to speak than the know-it-all who is behind in his installment payments.

Anyway, it's worth a test. If you'll follow my suggestions for the next year, you'll be a different person, living a rich, rewarding, and meaningful life. Four things, all of them simple.

One, remember that our rewards in life will be in exact proportion to our service.

Two, by giving your work a larger percentage of your capabilities and talents, you will, you must, increase your income substantially.

Three, since our lives depend on others, treat others in every facet of your life exactly as you want others to treat you. If you expect others to give you excellent products and services for the money you and your family spend, then you should make certain that your job is handled as excellently as it is possible for you, since it is the money of others that pays your salary.

Four, try to find some way every day in which your work can be improved. And above all, know your boss. He's the customer. Treat him with the respect, care, courtesy, and good humor he deserves. Remember, he pays all your bills every month. He will buy everything you will ever own. He may be coarse, crude, ignorant, selfish, conniving, and a thoroughgoing savage. He often will be. Here it is more important than ever that you treat him with all the care and attention you can muster. If you don't and if you permit his attitude to affect yours, you're admitting that he's the stronger person. If you respond the same way he conducts himself, you're admitting you're no better than he is.

Most people, however, are nice people. They're people like you and me who want to be liked and want to get along, who want to be friends. They have problems and sorrows of their own about which we're not aware. They have bad days and disappointments. Make sure that the time they're with you is a high spot in their day and that they'll want to come back, not just because of your company, but because of you.

If you'll do these things for a year, you'll be surprised and delighted, and you'll find you wouldn't live any other way for the world. If you're already living this way, you know what I mean.

Follow these steps for one year and you will be a different person, living a rich, rewarding, and meaningful life:

• Remember that your rewards in life are in exact proportion to your service. Increase your service to others and your rewards will increase in proportion.
• Give your work a larger percent of your capabilities and talents to serve "the boss."
• Treat others in every facet of your life as you want others to treat you.

1. If you expect others to give you excellent products and services for the money you and your family earn, make certain that your job is handled as excellently as it is possible for you.

2. Find some way every day in which your work can be improved to benefit "the boss."

Chapter 19

What Is Your Intermediate Goal?

Did you ever see Jack Nicklaus play golf? He was a golfing phenomenon never before seen in the world of golf, winning more major championships and money than any other golfer who ever lived. Yet if you watch him carefully, you can learn more than how to lower your handicap. You can learn a key strategy for success.

Each time Jack got ready to hit the ball, he'd have an intermediate aiming point, just a short distance from the ball. This intermediate aiming point was on line with the route he wanted the ball to travel. He would look down the fairway toward the green, then at the intermediate aiming point, then at the ball. His first task was to get the ball to pass over the intermediate point. If it did that, it would probably land very near the point on the fairway or green he had selected. It was always interesting watching his head and eyes move to the intermediate point, then to the distant point, then back to the intermediate point and back to the ball.

When he was ready, and not a moment before, he would uncork that legendary swing that left the gallery gasping and whooping with admiration and wonder. The ball would compress flat and be off and away on its considerable journey. It was the same with his short irons near the green. He always had an intermediate point with which he could line up his club head and the ball. We need intermediate aiming points, too, before we can successfully reach a substantial distant goal.

To write a book, one must write the first chapter, then the second, then the third, and so on. The book is first in outline form. The chapters are roughly sketched as to subject matter and content. One can get a mental picture of the book in final form with its color dust jacket coming from the printer; that's the goal. But first, there's that first chapter, then the second, and so on. Each chapter must be successfully completed as an integral part of the project before the project is complete.

And it's much the same with our big goals. All we can see is it as completed, with ourselves right in the middle of it. There we are; the job's done. That's where we want to land. But first there are the intermediate points to successfully complete. And it's the intermediate points that often prove too much or too difficult or too time consuming for the person to spend all that time completing and polishing. These are often the core skills, vital to the completion of the final project. Here we find the person who wants to amaze a friend through his skill at the piano but doesn't want to put in the time and effort to learn to play. This is the person who's forever looking for shortcuts. He or she daydreams, but when it comes down to the nitty-gritty of the intermediate goals, ah, that's too hard or boring or time consuming. Want to write books? How about mastering the language first? Want to get rich in real estate? Study the business first.

The first step of the successful person is commitment. There are no ifs or buts about it. He or she is fully 100 percent committed to the achievement of the goal and willing to take whatever intermediate steps are required. When bridges are burned, there's no escape route on which to come tiptoeing back when things get rough.

Commitment to all the intermediate goals, 100 percent. When that happens, the goal is as good as accomplished.

Chapter 20

Success: A Worthy Destination

It's been said that Americans can have anything they want. The trouble is, most don't know what they want, and so they drift through life taking circumstances as they come and settle for "good enough." Yet, 5 percent of the population does achieve an unusual level of success. And here is their secret.

The stories of people achieving unusual success despite all manner of handicaps never fail to capture our attention. They're inspirational to be sure. But they're much more than that if we study them closely. The boy whose legs were terribly burned and who was told he'd be lucky to ever walk again becomes a champion track star. The woman blind and deaf from infancy becomes one of the most inspirational figures of the century. And the poor children who rise to fame and fortune have nearly become commonplace.

In this age of unprecedented immigration, we see examples of people who start off in this world with virtually nothing and within a surprisingly short time have become wonderfully successful.

What sets these people apart, people with vast handicaps such as not knowing the language, not knowing the right people, not having any money? What drives the boy with the burned legs who becomes the champion runner or a Helen Keller, blind and deaf who becomes one of the most inspirational figures of our time? The answer, if fully understood, will bring you and me anything and everything we truly want, and it's deceptively simple. Perhaps it's too simple.

The people we've talked about here and the thousands currently doing the same thing all over the world are in possession of something the average person doesn't have. They have goals. They have a burning desire to succeed despite all obstacles and handicaps. They know exactly what they want; they think about it every day of their lives. It gets them up in the morning, and it keeps them giving their very best all day long. It's the last thing they think about before dropping off to sleep at night. They have a vision of exactly what they want to do, and that vision carries them over every obstacle.

This vision, this dream, this goal, invisible to all the world except the person holding it, is responsible for perhaps every great advance and achievement of humankind. It's the underlying motive for just about everything we see about us. Everything worthwhile achieved by men and women is a dream come true, a goal reached. It's been said that what the mind can conceive and believe, it can achieve.

It's the fine building where before there was an empty lot or an old eyesore. It's the bridge spanning the bay. It's landing on the moon. And it's that little convenience store in Midtown Manhattan. It's the lovely home on a tree-shaded street and the young person accepting the diploma. It's a low golf handicap and a position reached in the world of business. It's a certain income attained or amount of money invested. What the mind can conceive and believe, it can achieve.

We become what we think about. And when we're possessed by an exciting goal, we reach it. That's why it's been said, "Be choosy, therefore, of what you set your heart upon. For if you want it strongly enough, you'll get it."

Americans can have anything they want. The trouble is they don't know what they want. Oh, they want little things. They want a new car; they get it. They want a new refrigerator; they get it. They want a new home and they get it. The system never fails for them, but they don't seem to understand that it is a system. Nor that if it'll work for a refrigerator or a new car, it will work for anything else they want very much, just as well.

Goals are the very basis of any success. It is in fact the definition of success. The best definition of success I've ever found goes like this, "Success is the progressive realization of a worthy goal." Or in some cases the pursuit of a worthy "ideal." It's a beautiful definition of success. It means that anyone who's on course toward the fulfillment of a goal is successful.

Now, success doesn't lie in the achievement of a goal, although that's what the world considers success; it lies in the journey toward the goal. We're successful as long as we're working toward something we want to bring about in our lives. That's when the human being is at his or her best. That's what Cervantes meant when he wrote, "The road is better than the inn." We're at our best when we're climbing, thinking, planning, working, when we're on the road toward something we want to bring about.

With our definition, success being the progressive realization of a worthy goal, we cover all the bases. The young person working to finish school is as successful as any person on earth. The person working toward a particular position with his or her company is just as successful. If you have a goal that you find worthy of you as a person, a goal that fills you with joy at the thought of it, believe me, you'll reach it. But as you draw near and see that the goal will soon be achieved, begin to think ahead to the next goal you're going to set. It often happens that a writer halfway through a book will hit upon the idea for his next one and begin making notes or ideas for a title even while he's finishing work on the one in progress. That's the way it should be.

It's estimated that about 5% of the population achieves unusual success. For the rest, average seems to be good enough. Most seem to just drift along, taking circumstances as they come, and perhaps hoping from time to time that things will get better.

I like to compare human beings with ships, as Carlyle used to do. It's estimated that about 95 percent can be compared to ships without rudders, subject to every shift of wind and tide. They're helplessly adrift, and while they fondly hope that they will one day drift into some rich and bustling port, for every narrow harbor entrance, there are 1,000 miles of rocky coastline. The chances of their drifting into port are 1,000 to 1 against them. Our state lottery is a tax on such people. So are the slot machines in Las Vegas and Atlantic City. Someone wins from time to time to be sure, but the odds are still there... stacked steeply against them.

But the 5 percent who have taken the time and exercised the discipline to climb into the driver's seat of their lives, who've decided upon a challenging goal to reach and have fully committed themselves to reaching it, sail straight and far across the deep oceans of life, reaching one port after another and accomplishing more in just a few years than the rest accomplish in a lifetime.

If you should visit a ship in port and ask the captain for his next port of call, he'll tell you in a single sentence. Even though the captain cannot see his port, his destination for fully 99% of the voyage, he knows it's there. And then, barring an unforeseen and highly unlikely catastrophe, he'll reach it. If someone asks you for your next port of call, your goal, could you tell him? Is your goal clean and concise in your mind? Do you have it written down? It's a good idea. We need reminding, reinforcement. If you can get a picture of your goal and stick it to your bathroom mirror, it's an excellent idea to do so. Thousands of successful people carry their goals written on a card in their wallets or purses.

When you ask people what they're working for, chances are they'll answer in vague generalities. They might say, "Oh, good health or happiness or lots of money." That's not good enough. Good health should be a universal goal. We all want that, and do our best to achieve and maintain it. Happiness is a byproduct of something else. And lots of money is much too vague. It might work, but I think it's better to choose a particular sum of money. The better, the clearer our goal is defined, the more real it becomes to us, and before long, the more attainable.

Happiness comes from the direction in which we're moving. Children are happier on Christmas morning before opening their presents than they are Christmas afternoon. No matter how wonderful their presents may be, it's after Christmas. They'll enjoy their gifts, to be sure, but we often find them querulous and irritable Christmas afternoon. We're happier on our way out to dinner than we are on the way home. We're happier going on vacation than we are coming home from it. And we're happier moving toward our goals than even after they've been accomplished, believe it or not.

Life plays no favorites. Yet of one thing you may be sure, you will become what you think about. If your thinking is circular and chaotic, your life will reflect that chaos. But if your thinking is orderly and clear, if you have a goal that's important for you to reach, then reach it you will. One goal at a time. That's important. That's where most people unwittingly make their mistake. They don't concentrate on a single goal long enough to reach it before they're off on another track, then another, with the result that they achieve nothing. Nothing but confusion and excuses.

By thinking every morning, every night, and as many times during the day as you can about this exciting single goal you've established for yourself, you actually begin moving toward it and bringing it toward you. When you concentrate your thinking, it's like taking a river that's twisting and turning and meandering all over the countryside and putting it into a straight, smooth channel. Now it has power, direction, economy, speed.

So decide upon your goal. Insist upon it. Demand it! Look at your goal card every morning and night and as many times during the day as you conveniently can. By so doing, you will insinuate your goal into your subconscious mind. You'll see yourself as having already attained your goal, and do that every day without fail, and it will become a habit before you realize it. A habit that will take you from one success to another all the years of your life. For that is the secret of success, the door to everything you will ever have or be.

You are now and you most certainly will become... what you think about.

Uncover Your Primary Goal

If you are like so many millions who don't know what it is you want sufficiently to name as your primary goal, I recommend you make out a want list. Take a notepad, go off by yourself, and write down the things you'd really like to have or do very much. One might be a beautiful new home or a trip around the world, a visit to some special country or place. It might be a yearning for a sailboat or motor yacht, or if you're an avid fisherman, you might want to go salmon fishing in Alaska or trout fishing in New Zealand. It might be a business of your own or a particular position with your company. It might be a certain income that will permit you to live the way you'd like to live. Or, a certain amount of money in good investments or in a savings account. How about a special make of car? Or an addition to your present home? Just write down everything you can think of that you would really like to see come about in your life. Then when you've exhausted your wants, go over the list again and number the items in the order of their importance, and make number one your present goal.

Chapter 21

Fake It Till You Make It

THE MUNDANE LITTLE THINGS YOU DO TODAY WHILE PREPARING FOR TOMORROW'S SUCCESS MAY WELL BE THE THINGS THAT GUARANTEE THAT SUCCESS. GIVE IT YOUR BEST - ALWAYS.

When I was an announcer/writer at radio station KTAR in Phoenix, Arizona, my goal was to become a network announcer in Chicago or New York, the national headquarters of radio at that time. I listened to the network announcers and practiced reading commercials as they did so that the copy sounded spontaneous and ad-libbed. I studied the delivery of every first-class network announcer in the country, and soon I could sound very much like them. Every commercial I read on the air at KTAR, whether for the local mortuary or sporting goods store, I read as though it were a national commercial for the most world-renowned company.

I gave so much pizzazz to the local commercials my announcer friends soon dubbed me "network" and kidded me - found my efforts ludicrous. They were helping me on my way. "Why do you knock yourself out on those ridiculous commercials?" they'd ask. And I would smile and go about my business.

I would listen every day to those men and women who were at the very top of my field, and no matter how mundane the copy or humble a place of business, when I stepped up to the microphone, I had a picture of the entire country listening to every word I spoke. *I gave it my very best - always.*

And after 21 years of KTAR in Phoenix, I felt I was ready for the big time. I told my friends I'd soon quit and head for Chicago. My announcement was met with unbelieving stares and the most vociferous arguments. "There are 450 union card-carrying announcers walking the streets of Chicago trying to get work in the big stations there, " I was told. But my mind was made up, and I bought a one-way ticket to Chicago.

In Chicago I took a room at the old Chicagoan Hotel in the Loop, bought a copy of the *Chicago Tribune,* and turned on my portable radio. There were two target radio stations. They were the two biggest and the best at the time, WBBM CBS in the Wrigley Building on Michigan Avenue, and WMAQ NBC in the Merchandise Mart. I tackled WBBM first. I'll never forget that first day in those beautiful, posh surroundings. The marble floors, the uniformed elevator starters, those fabulous brass and glistening hardwood elevators.

Al Morey was program director at the time. He was most cordial and immediately led me to a large nearby studio for an audition. He gave me a fist full of copy that included some tricky commercials and part of a newscast.

The studio was as impressive as the rest of the place, very large for one thing, with a concert grand piano and sound effects paraphernalia. I walked to the standing microphone and looked into the darkened engineer's room beyond the slanting glass. There was an old-time engineer, and Al Morey nodded his head and threw me a hand cue, and I began.

After my interview he told me he'd let me know, and the next day I repeated the process at WMAQ. Then I waited. Finally, Al Morey called. I not only had the job, I was under contract for more money than I had dreamed of earning. My 21 years of doing network commercials for a local radio station had paid off, and I was now a CBS network announcer on a station whose coverage blanketed most of the Midwestern United States, to say nothing of the country's second largest metropolitan market.

Indeed, I had arrived. I was giddy with a sudden inflation of my self-esteem. I was a passable writer, and I could hold my own with any announcer in the country. I was off and running. My preparation had paid off. Where were all those 450 unemployed union card-carrying announcers?

Chapter 22

It's Not the Destination

In the great Greek poem by Constantine Cavafy titled "Ithaka," we are reminded that it is the voyage and the adventures on the way that count, not the arrival itself.

This seems to be a most difficult truth to understand. This is not to say that a person's goal in life is unimportant. On the contrary, it's vital. For without a goal, a distant destination, we would not be on the trip at all. Instead we'd run around in circles, endlessly following the shoreline around our tiny island. Every person needs a great and distant goal toward which to strive. But in traveling toward it, he should try to keep in mind that the fabled land he seeks has shores much like the one he left behind and that its purpose is not so much a resting place but, rather, the reason for the trip.

Where a person goes is not nearly as important as how he gets there. That a house is built is not all that important. It is the manner in which it is built that makes it great, average, or poor. That we live is not nearly as important as the manner in which we live.

Misunderstanding this often keeps people in a state of unhappiness and anxiety. They forget to enjoy the trip. They forget what they're really looking for, or what they should be looking for: the discovery of themselves. This is the island toward which everyone should journey. It's a difficult journey, beset, like the travels of Ulysses, with many dangers and hardships. But it gives real meaning to life, and there are many rich rewards to be found along the way - all kinds of serendipitous benefits.

It means asking the questions that are hard to answer: *Where am I going? Why am I going there? What do I really want, and why do I want it? Am I gradually realizing my potential? Am I discovering my best talents and abilities and using them to their fullest? Am I living fully extended in my one chance at life on earth? Am I really living? Who am I?*

These are the questions everyone must ask himself and answer. As Emerson said, "Though we travel the world over to find the beautiful, we must carry it with us, or we find it not."

Whatever you're looking for must first be found within you, whether it be peace, happiness, riches, or great accomplishments. Everything we do outwardly is only an expression of what we are inwardly. To ask for anything else is as absurd as looking for apples on an oak tree.

So the person who knows what he wants, knows what he must become, and he then fixes his attention on the preparation and development of himself. As he grows toward the ideal he holds in his mind, he finds interest, zest, and joy on the journey. He looks forward to tomorrow, but he also enjoys today, for it is the tomorrow he looked forward to yesterday. He knows that if he cannot find meaning and value in his present, he will very likely be missing it in his future. Today is the future of five years ago. Are you enjoying it as much as you thought you would? Have you progressed to the point you wanted then to reach?

Chapter 23

Acres of Diamonds

Every kind of work has enormous opportunity lurking within it. The opportunities are there now, clamoring to be noticed. But they cannot speak or print signs for us to read. Our part of the bargain is to look at our work with "intelligent objectivity". If we have the wisdom and patience to intelligently, effectively explore the work in which we're now engaged, to explore ourselves, we would most likely find the riches we seek.

The story - a true one - is told of an African farmer who heard tales about other farmers who had made millions by discovering diamond mines. These tales so excited the farmer that he could hardly wait to sell his farm and go prospecting for diamonds himself. He sold the farm and spent the rest of his life wandering the African continent searching unsuccessfully for the gleaming gems that brought such high prices on the markets of the world. Finally, worn out and in a fit of despondency, he threw himself into a river and drowned.

Meanwhile, the man who had bought his farm happened to be crossing the small stream on the property one day, when suddenly there was a bright flash of blue and red light from the stream bottom. He bent down and picked up a stone. It was a good-sized stone, and admiring it, he brought it home and put it on his fireplace mantel as an interesting curiosity.

Several weeks later a visitor picked up the stone, looked closely at it, hefted it in his hand, and nearly fainted. He asked the farmer if he knew what he'd found. When the farmer said, no, that he thought it was a piece of crystal, the visitor told him he had found one of the largest diamonds ever discovered.

The farmer had trouble believing that. He told the man that his creek was full of such stones, not all as large as the one on the mantel, but sprinkled generously throughout the creek bottom.

The farm the first farmer had sold, so that he might find a diamond mine, turned out to be one of the most productive diamond mines on the entire African continent. The first farmer had owned, free and clear... acres of diamonds. But he had sold them for practically nothing, in order to look for them elsewhere. The moral is clear: If the first farmer had only taken the time to study and prepare himself to learn what diamonds looked like in their rough state, and to thoroughly explore the property he had before looking elsewhere, all of his wildest dreams would have come true.

The thing about this story that has so profoundly affected millions of people is the idea that each of us is, at this very moment, standing in the middle of our own acres of diamonds. If we had only had the wisdom and patience to intelligently and effectively explore the work in which we're now engaged, to explore ourselves, we would most likely find the riches we seek, whether they be financial or intangible or both.

Before you go running off to what you think are greener pastures, make sure that your own is not just as green or perhaps even greener. *It has been said that if the other guy's pasture appears to be greener than ours, it's quite possible that it's getting better care.* Besides, while you're looking at other pastures, other people are looking at yours.

A man I knew in Arizona began with a small gas station. One day, while one of his young attendants filled a man's gas tank, he watched the customer while he stood about waiting for the job to be finished. It dawned upon him that the man had money in his pockets and there were things he needed or wanted that he would pay for if they were conveniently displayed where he could see them.

So he began adding things. Fishing tackle, then fishing licenses, hunting and camping equipment, rifles, shot guns, ammunition, hunting licenses. He found an excellent line of aluminum fishing boats and trailers. He began buying up the contiguous property around him. Then he added an auto parts department. He always sold cold soft drinks and candy, but now he added an excellent line of chocolates in a refrigerated case. Before long, he sold more chocolates than anyone else in the state. He carried thousands of things his customers could buy while waiting for their cars to be serviced.

All the products he sold also guaranteed that most of the gas customers in town would come to his station. He sold more gas. He began cashing checks on Friday, and his sales grew. It all started with a man with a human brain watching a customer standing around with money in his pockets and nothing to spend it on. Others would have lived and died with the small service station, and they do. My friend saw the diamonds.

Many service station operators, upon seeing a wealthy customer drive in, might say to themselves, *I ought to be in his business.* Not so. There's just as much opportunity in one business as another, if we'll only stop playing copycat and begin to think creatively, in new directions. It's there; believe me. And it's your job to find it.

Take the time to stand off and look at your work as a stranger might and ask, *Why does he do it that way? Has he noticed how what he's doing might be capitalized upon or multiplied?* If you're happy with things as they are, then by all means, keep them that way. But there's great fun in finding diamonds hiding in ourselves and in our work. We never get bored or blasé or find ourselves in a rut. A rut, remember, is really nothing more than a grave with the ends kicked out. Some of the most interesting businesses in the world grew out of what was originally a very small idea in a very small area. If something is needed in one town, then the chances are it's also needed in all towns and cities all over the country.

You might also ask yourself, *How good am I at what I'm presently doing?* Do you know all there is to know about your work? Would you call yourself a first-class professional at your work? How would your work stand up against the work of others in your line?

The first thing we need to do to become a "diamond miner" is to break away from the crowd and quit assuming that because people in the millions are living that way, I must be the best way. It is not the best way. It's the average way. The people going the best way are way out in front. They're so far ahead of the crowd you can't even see their dust anymore. These are the people who live and work on the leading edge, the cutting edge, and they mark the way for all the rest.

It takes imagination, curious imagination, to know that diamonds don't look like cut and polished gemstones in their rough state, nor does a pile of iron ore look like stainless steel. To prospect your own acres of diamonds, develop a faculty we might call "intelligent objectivity." The faculty to stand off and look at your work as a person from Mars might look at it. Within the framework of what industry or profession does your job fall? Isn't it time for a refreshing change of some kind? How can the customer be given more value? Each morning ask yourself, *How can I increase my service today? There are rare and very marketable diamonds lurking all around me. Have I been looking for them? Have I examined every facet of my work and of the industry or profession in which it has its life?*

There are better ways to do what you are presently doing. What are they? How will your work be performed 20 years from now? Everything in the world is in a state of evolution and improvement. How could you do today what would eventually be done anyway?

Sure there's risk involved; there's no growth of any kind without risk. We start running risks when we get out of bed in the morning. Risks are good for us. They bring out the best that's in us. They brighten the eye and get the mind cooking. They quicken the step and put a new shining look on our days. Human beings should never be settled. It's okay for chickens and cows and cats, but it's wrong for human beings. People start to die when they become settled. We need to keep things stirred up.

Back in 1931, Lloyd C. Douglas, the world-famous novelist who wrote *The Robe, Magnificent Obsession,* and other best-selling books, wrote a magazine article titled "Escape." In that article Douglas asked, "Who of us has not at some time toyed briefly with the temptation to run away? If all the people who have given that idea the temporary hospitality of their imagination were to have acted upon it, few would be living at their present addresses. And of the small minority who did carry the impulse into effect, it's doubtful if many ever disengaged themselves as completely as they had hoped from the problems that hurled them forth. More often than otherwise, it may be surmised, they packed up their troubles in their old kit bags and took them along. "

The point of the article was simply, don't try to run away from your troubles.
Overcome them. Prevail right where you are. What we're really after is not escape from our complexities and frustrations, but a triumph over them. And one of the best ways to accomplish

that is to get on course and stay there. Restate and reaffirm your goal, the thing you want most to do, the place in life you want most to reach. See it clearly in your mind's eye just as you can envision the airport in Los Angeles when you board your plane in New York. Like a great ship in a storm, just keep your heading and your engines running. The storm will pass, although sometimes it seems that it never will. One bright morning you'll find yourself passing the harbor light.

Then you can give a big sigh of relief and rest a while, and almost before you know it, you'll find your eyes turning seaward again. You'll think of a new harbor you'd like to visit, a new voyage upon which to embark. And once again, you'll set out.

That's just the way this funny-looking, two-legged, curious, imaginative, tinkering, fiddling dreamer called a human being operates. He escapes from problems not by running away from them, but by overcoming them. And no sooner does he overcome one set of problems, but he starts looking around for new and more difficult pickles to get into and out of.

If you feel like running away from it all once in a while, you're perfectly normal. If you stay and get rid of your problems by working your way through them, you're a success. Start taking an hour a day with a legal pad and dissect your work. Take it apart and look at its constituent parts. There's opportunity there. That's your acre of diamonds.

DIAMOND MINING

To prospect your own acres of diamonds and unearth the opportunities that exist in your life right now, regularly challenge yourself with some key questions:

1. How good am I at what I'm presently doing?

2. Can I call myself a first-class professional at my work?

3. How would my work stand up against the work of others in my field?

4. Do I know all I can about my industry or profession?

5. How can the customer be given a better break?

6. How can I increase my service?

7. There are rare and very marketable diamonds lurking all around me. Have I been looking for them? Have I examined every facet of my work and of the industry or profession in which it has its life?

8. There are better ways to do what I'm presently doing. What are they?

9. How will my work be performed 20 years from now?

10. Everything in the world is in a state of evolution and improvement.
How can I do now what will eventually be done anyway?

Chapter 24

Don't Follow the Follower

95 percent of people never succeed because they're following the wrong group.

Processionary caterpillars travel in long, undulating lines, one creature behind the other. Jean Hanri Fabre, the French entomologist, once lead a group of these caterpillars onto the rim of a large flowerpot so that the leader of the procession found himself nose to tail with the last caterpillar in the procession, forming a circle without end or beginning.

Through sheer force of habit and, of course, instinct, the ring of caterpillars circled the flowerpot for seven days and seven nights, until they died from exhaustion and starvation. An ample supply of food was close at hand and plainly visible, but it was outside the range of the circle, so the caterpillars continued along the beaten path.

People often behave in a similar way. Habit patterns and ways of thinking become deeply established, and it seems easier and more comforting to follow them than to cope with change, even when that change may represent freedom, achievement, and success.

If someone shouts, "Fire!" it is automatic to blindly follow the crowd, and many thousands have needlessly died because of it. How many stop to ask themselves: Is this really the best way out of here?

So many people "miss the boat" because it's easier and more comforting to follow - to follow without questioning the qualifications of the people just ahead - than to do some independent thinking and checking.

A hard thing for most people to fully understand is that people in such numbers can be so wrong, like the caterpillars going around and around the edge of the flowerpot, with life and food just a short distance away. If most people are living that way, it must be right, they think. But a little checking will reveal that throughout all recorded history the majority of mankind has an unbroken record of being wrong about most things, especially important things. For a time we thought the earth was flat and later we thought the sun, stars, and planets traveled around the Earth. Both ideas are now considered ridiculous, but at the time they were believed and defended by the vast majority of followers. In the hindsight of history we must have looked like those caterpillars blindly following the follower out of habit rather than stepping out of line to look for the truth.

It's difficult for people to come to the understanding that only a small minority of people ever really get the word about life, about living abundantly and successfully. Success in the important departments of life seldom comes naturally, no more naturally than success at anything - a musical instrument, sports, fly-fishing, tennis, golf, business, marriage, parenthood.

But for some reason most people wait passively for success to come to them - like the caterpillars going around in circles, waiting for sustenance, following nose to tail - living as other people are living in the unspoken, tacit assumption that other people know how to live successfully.

It's a good idea to step out of the line every once in a while and look around to see if the line is going where we want it to go.

If it is not, it might be time for a new leader and a new direction.

Falling Isn't Failing ... Unless You Fail to Get Up

For those who have tried repeatedly to break a habit of some kind, only to repeatedly fail, Mary Pickford said, "Falling is not failing, unless you fail to get up." Most people who finally win the battle over a habit they have wanted to change have done so only after repeated failures. And it's the same with most things.

The breaking of a longtime habit does seem like the end of the road at the time - the complete cessation of enjoyment. Suddenly dropping the habit so fills our minds with the desire for the old habitual way that, for a while, it seems there will no longer be any peace, any sort of enjoyment. But that's not true. New habits form in a surprisingly short time, and a whole new world opens up to us.

So, if you've been trying to start in a new direction, you might do well to remember the advice of Mary Pickford: breaking an old habit isn't the end of the road; it's just a bend in the road. And falling isn't failing, unless you don't get up.

Chapter 25

The Difference Between the 'Haves' & the 'Have Nots'

Meet two kinds of people - the "Haves" and "Have Nots" - and the one decision that separates them.

I once had occasion to visit Charleston, South Carolina. I had never been there before, so I hired a taxi to drive me around the historic old town. I particularly wanted to see the Battery, where the famous shot was fired on Fort Sumpter. Along this beautiful drive, some of Charleston's oldest and finest homes look out over the bay. I commented to my cab driver on what lovely homes they were, and he said, "Yeah, some of those homes have 40 rooms." Then he thought for a moment and said, "And every one of them is owned by a crook."

The truth was those homes were built by the men and women who made the largest contribution to the city of Charleston. But that is how the Have Nots of the world justify themselves and their lot in life. They think people who earn the big money that allows them to enjoy luxurious lifestyles are crooks, lucky, endowed with more brains or talents, privy to occult secrets, or born into wealth. Yet these are only excuses.

People who fail to make the grade financially are seldom honest enough to admit that they really didn't try and keep trying. So in order to justify their failure or mediocre lives, they dream up and pass along these excuses.

I've discovered that the only difference between the people who earn big incomes and those who earn small incomes is that those earning big incomes *decided* to earn more. Without the decision to earn more, you can't possibly think of ways to increase your income.

This decision is the simple, yet elusive, difference between the Haves and the Have Nots. The moment you *decide* to go after wealth, success, or anything you desire in life, that is when you will start thinking about ways to accomplish it.

What's more, you cannot simply make the decision once and then relax. You must make the commitment again and again, and continually overcome your fears to turn back toward safety.

The Have Nots do not want to do more than they have to - and that is why they continue to "have not."

Growth can feel uncomfortable, as it pushes us to step out of our comfort zone - to do more than what's required of us. This is the trap of the Have Nots, and it is why so few people commit to the decision to become Haves.

I remember reading that the employees at Macy's department store in New York had grumbled because the company had been hiring executives and managers from outside the company. So Macy's management put in a free management-training program for its employees so that it could promote from within the organization. However, only about 3 percent took advantage of the training, even though it was free. All they had to do was stay after work for a few hours.

Similarly, only about 3 percent of all American armed force veterans have taken advantage of their GI Bill educational allowances.

That 3 percent figure keeps popping up in cases like that. It seems that only about 3 percent of people are seriously interested in investing a part of their time and energy in programs to help them get ahead in the world. The rest yell and flail around for pay raises and more fringe benefits. But when it's suggested that they might do something to improve themselves, make themselves more valuable, they don't want to do it.

Success is available to everyone who commits to being successful.

I hope you'll decide to become a Have person. If you've read this far, you have probably already made that essential decision. Here are the next steps:

1. Start getting up a little earlier than you're accustomed to. This gives you extra time that 95 percent of the people in this world are not using at all. One hour earlier a day gives you six extra 40-hour weeks a year. During this extra hour, take a refreshing shower, dress, get yourself a fresh, hot cup of coffee or tea, and then sit down to a clean sheet of paper.

2. Decide what you want in life. More wealth? Success? Happiness? More time with your family? At the top of the paper write down your goals. For example, let's say you write down the amount of money per year that you intend to earn soon. That's your financial goal. You don't have to tell anyone. It's nobody's business but yours.

3. Start to think. Think about your goal and what it will mean to you and your family. See how many ideas you can come up with to help you reach that goal, ideas to improve what you now do for a living. Ways of increasing your contribution to match your income goal.

4. Try for five ideas every morning. Write them down and save those sheets of paper in a special "ideas" file. Focus on ideas within your line of work or expertise or area that you are most interested in. To think well and profitably, you must discipline your thinking. Keep your thoughts on course, controlled, and focused. Many or perhaps most of your ideas will prove fruitless. But some of them will be very good. A few will be excellent. And every once in a while you'll come up with something truly outstanding.

5. Develop a sense of expectancy. That is, try to hold the feeling that the goal you're shooting for is a sure thing and that it's only a matter of time before it's realized. Henry Ford didn't start making cars until he was 45. A friend of mine started a new company at 65. He's still going strong, and his new company has sales of better than $300 million a year. It's never too late.

6. Change your attitude. *Attitude* has been called the most important word in the language. William James put it this way: "The greatest discovery of my generation is that human beings can alter their lives by altering their attitudes of mind." To change your attitude, begin to act like the person you most want to become. If you were already in possession of the goal you're shooting for, how would you conduct yourself in all of your affairs? How would you dress? How would you talk? Well, do it now, and tomorrow, and the next day. Begin now to act the part of the person you most want to become. And you will end up becoming that person. The German philosopher Goethe gave us the secret when he said, "Before you can do something, you must first *be* something."

Practice your new attitude every day - every waking hour. Practice focused thinking a few minutes every morning and you'll find yourself thinking all day long.

The late renowned psychologist Dr. Abraham Maslow found that people who live close to their true capacity have a pronounced sense of well being and considerable energy. They see themselves as leading purposeful and creative lives. Isn't that what we all want to do? I believe it is. And it all begins the moment you *decide* to become a Have person and leave the Have Nots to their complaints and excuses.

Five ideas a day is 25 a week if you don't think on weekends. That's more than 1,000 ideas a year. One idea can get you to that income you're shooting for. The law of averages swings so far in your favor you just can't miss.

There are two kinds of people: the Haves and the Have Nots. The Have Nots think the only people who earn large incomes resulting in successful, luxury lifestyles are crooks, lucky, endowed with more brains or talents, privy to occult secrets, or born into wealth. These are only alibis, a way for the Have Nots to justify their failure or mediocre lives. Learn the secrets to a successful life among the Haves and leave the Have Nots to their complaints and their alibis.

Chapter 26

The Flame of Hope

Every person is born with the basic drive to persevere. No matter how crushed, how defeated, how demoralized, when all hope seems gone, there is, in the healthy person, a small, indistinguishable flame of hope - like a faint but persistent pilot light that stays alight, much like the fire ancient man used to carry with him as he moved from place to place.

Almost everyone comes to a place in life when going on seems futile, even ridiculous - when he seems overwhelmed by a suffocating mattress of events and situations, and desires just to sit down in the middle of the road and let the world and everything in it go to blazes.

So he sits down for a while. But then the vibration of the world seems to make itself felt in his bones. Pretty soon, he raises his head and begins to look around. After a while, he takes a couple of deep breaths, gets slowly, painfully to his feet, wobbles there for a minute or two, and then he starts out again. Often as not, around the next bend in the road, he'll find the reason he kept going. And he'll shudder at the thought of how close he came to giving up.

His hope lies in movement and time. If he does not get up and start moving again, he's done for. But he has this natural drive to keep moving along the road. As long as he keeps heading for what he's looking for, what seemed like the end of the world for him will be nothing more than a bad dream, and a part of the preparation he needed to qualify for the achievement his perseverance has brought.

Movement, time, and the law of averages; I remember reading about the manager of a major-league ball club who kept a rookie on the team and in the lineup because even though he wasn't hitting anywhere near what was expected of him, when he struck out, he struck out swinging. He wasn't just standing there watching strikes go by. And, as the manager expected, he soon started getting wood on the ball and bringing his average up to where it belonged.

Discouragement seems to be part of life, but the reason people prevail is because of this built-in drive to keep going.

Chapter 27

Nine Steps for Solving Any Problem

For any problem, no matter how big or complex it may be, there is a solution. Use these nine steps to find it!

What are the similarities in problem solving, decision-making, and goal achievement? Actually, they're alike in many ways. A decision that must be made is little more than a problem awaiting a solution. We might even call it a simple problem. When we're faced with a decision, we rarely have to choose between more than two or three alternatives, whereas, in solving a problem, we sometimes face what seems to be an endless list of possibilities. And, what about goal achievement? Isn't a goal a point we wish to reach? The problem is to move from where we are now, to where we want to be. So, problem solving, decision-making, and goal achievement are all closely related functions of creative thinking. It's important that we keep this in mind.

The first step in solving any problem is to define it. You should always be sure you understand a problem before you go to work on its solution.

Next, you should write down everything you know about the problem. This information might come from your own experience, from books that contain
background and statistical data, the Internet, or from friends and business associates who know something about the area in which the problem lies.

Third, decide whom to see. List the names of people and organizations that are recognized authorities on the problem.

This is your opportunity to go "all out" for the facts. After determining who can help you, contact them, talk with them, and pick their brains for all the information they possess that can help you solve the problem.

After doing this, be sure to make a note of each thing that's germane to the problem. Don't risk forgetting anything that could help you find the solution.

The fifth step in solving a problem creatively is called "Individual Ideation." This is personal "brainstorming," or thinking with the brakes of judgment off! Don't try to decide whether an idea is good or bad - just write it down the moment it comes to you. You can pick and choose - what you're after is a lot of ideas.

Remember the four rules for brainstorming: (1) No negative thinking; (2) The wilder the ideas, the better; (3) A large number of ideas is essential; and (4) Combination and improvement of ideas is what you're after.

One idea often leads to another, better idea. Don't worry if some of your ideas seem far-fetched or impractical. You're looking for all the ideas you can possibly find. Don't reject any - write them all down!

Then Group Brainstorm. This is your opportunity to put the minds of others to work on the problem. Handle this session the same way you did your "Individual Ideation." No negative thinking, no criticism at this stage; the wilder the ideas the better; get as many ideas as possible; and, try for idea combination and improvement. Write down all the ideas the group comes up with.

When you have all your ideas written down, rate them for effectiveness and facility. The effectiveness scale ranges from "very effective" to "probably effective" to "doubtful." And the facility scale ranges from "easy" to "not so easy" to "difficult." The rating of ideas will clearly indicate the likely success of any possible solution. Of course, it's best to consider first the idea or ideas that are rated both "very effective" and "easy."

Suppose you're a manufacturer. And suppose your sales and marketing team brainstorming comes up with some ideas to increase sales. Let's say one of the ideas is to revamp completely one of the products that your company is offering to the public. Let's rate this idea in terms of effectiveness. You know the present product meets a need and is acceptable to the buying public. What about an entirely changed product? Without a lot of marketing tests and then a period of actual manufacturing for sale, it would be hard to say just how effective this idea would be in increasing sales. Better rate it "doubtful."

And how does this idea of completely revamping one of the products check out in the facility area - "easy," "not so easy," or "difficult"? It would be "difficult," wouldn't it? It would require new engineering, new tools, new manufacturing plans, new packaging, and new marketing methods.

Suppose, however, that one of the salesperson's ideas is to run TV advertisements for the company's product on one of the major television networks. This would be "probably effective" and would be "not so easy," but it could be done.

Let's say another idea is to set up a new sales incentive program, a program directed to those people who are at the front of the problem, the salespeople. If it were a well-designed and implemented incentive program with predictable compensation for increased performance, it would stand a good chance of being "very effective." It would be relatively "easy" to do. It should increase the company's sales.

There are many other evaluation yardsticks you might use. Two more are time and money. Try rating your ideas against these measurements. For example, in the case of a manufacturer who wants to increase its sales, certainly to change the product would take a great deal of time and money. And to advertise it on a popular network television program would cost a great deal. On the other hand, to introduce a new sales incentive program might be neither too costly nor too time consuming.

Remember, when you evaluate your ideas, measure them against these four yardsticks: effectiveness, facility, time, and cost. Every idea you have may not be worth creative action, and that's why you must skillfully evaluate each of them. But once you've carefully judged your ideas, take action.

Enter your ideas into an "Action Plan": decide who should do it, when it should be done, when to start, and how to do it. These are all important considerations because the execution of the solution is just as important as the solution itself.

Be certain to give yourself a deadline for putting your plan into action. We work hardest and most efficiently when we know there is a definite time element involved. So, make a note of the date when you must put your solution to work. It's good to remember that timing is often critical when a new idea is introduced. Carefully calculate the deadline in the light of the general situation. You might write down a second date - the one by which you intend to have the action completed and the problem solved.

Remember what was said earlier about problem solving, decision-making, and goal achievement? They have a great deal in common. They can all be attacked in much the same way.

For any problem... no matter how big or complex it may be... there is a solution. All you have to do is find it! History is filled with people who believed a problem did not have a solution and they *did not* find it, and people who believed there was a solution and they *did* find it - same problem, different perspective, one successful and one not. Which type of person will you be?

Remember these steps for brainstorming your ideas:

1. Define the problem.
2. Write down everything you know about the problem.
3. Decide what people and resources to bring into the solution.
4. Make a note of everything that is germane to the problem.
5. Conduct a personal brainstorming Individual Ideation.
6. Utilize Group Brainstorming and rate your ideas for effectiveness, facility, time, and cost.
7. Evaluate your ideas for the best options.
8. Create an "Action Plan."
9. Give yourself a deadline for putting your plan into action.

Chapter 28

A Pain in the Colon

A Witty Play on Punctuation

The Mental Health Society has reported that over 43% of people who have nervous breakdowns come from affluent families. Undoubtedly then, the other 57% come from offices. It is not the clamor; it's the grammar. We're not permitted to dangle participles or solder split infinitives. Prepositions are to be pushed into the thick, never to the rear of things. When we play mating games, it's against the rules to match a singular subject with a plural verb. It's a mortal sin to separate the subject from the predicate by a comma. They may never get together again. And the person who doesn't know a plural possessive is a person who doesn't know where the "s" belongs.

If you cannot figure out when to use a semicolon or colon, use a period. The
semicolon is half the man the period is and twice the man the colon is. It is used in place of two short sentences with the same related thought. The semicolon can stop something, but it cannot maintain the stoppage. The colon is the stop, look, and listen sign that tells you to stop because there's something up ahead such as listed information. The benefit of using the colon is I), to save time, 2), to save space, and 3) to delineate the facts.

The comma is the sex symbol of the punctuating world. It is the emotion of the written sentence, the appealing little curve that people find so hard to resist. We get this irresistible urge to pick it up at the drop of a voice, at a lull in the conversation, and at a change of pace. It lies there so seductively waiting for its chance to break up phrases, come between words, and give expression to thoughts. Words such as *therefore, nevertheless,* and *however* gain strength from the comma. It's sometimes perceived, always follows them faithfully, and without the comma, these words would pale in insignificance. And no matter how much we misuse it, it's always there tempting us. The period is the end of a sentence, but never, never let the sentence end with a preposition. This is unforgivable. Something up with which employers will positively not put.

With all its humor and irony, this is an interesting little short course on punctuation for the millions who manage to get through school without quite figuring it out. Incidentally, I was just kidding about the dangling participle and the old myth about ending a sentence with a preposition. That went out with the one-room schoolhouse.

Chapter 29

Lloyd Conant: This I Believe

Lloyd Victor Conant had the vision to create a company with the sole purpose to empower people to succeed. He believed that in each of us lies the unawakened strength to live the life we most desire... and he was right. In this rare interview, learn this humble entrepreneur's powerful philosophies on service, teamwork, idea generation, and the journey to success - which have been the foundation of Nightingale-Conant for over 40 years.

The story of Lloyd Victor Conant, a brilliant entrepreneur who started a company founded with the dream to empower the world to succeed.

This is the story of a man who was born in the little town of St. Joseph, Missouri, and grew up believing that anyone lucky enough to be born in the United States could become anything he set his heart and mind upon. Of course, World War I1 came along, and although he had just married his sweetheart and there was a baby on the way, he went off to war and became a pilot and served in the European Theater.

After the war, he began selling business equipment and became especially interested in automatic typewriters. And so this young man journeyed to Chicago with his machines and the desire to make his fortune in the big city. It was very difficult for him and his family in the early days, but he stuck with it, maintained a healthy attitude and a good sense of humor, and gradually his business grew.

And it came to pass that I met this man in the early 1950s in Chicago, and we worked together on several projects. We found that we had similar interests, although entirely different talents and that we seemed to make a good team. So finally we merged our two small companies. He would handle the business end, at which he was very good and to which he was completely dedicated, and I would write and record the products we would sell.

The idea was that millions of people are too busy and don't have the specialized knowledge or time to go digging up the kind of information they need if they're to succeed and continue to grow as persons. So we tried to do that for them and put the ideas in a recorded form so that they could obtain the information while they were doing other things like commuting to and from work in their cars, exercising, or dressing in the morning. It was a great idea but being completely new, it grew slowly for the first 10 or 15 years.

Then, the company started to grow and eventually became very successful under this man's direction. He made his fortune all right. But he was so wrapped up in the business which he loved and the people who worked for him and with him, that he never left it.

This man, from St. Joseph, Missouri, was Lloyd Victor Conant, and he died on April 2, 1986. He was my partner for 30 years, and I miss him very much. The world is a better place because he lived and worked in it.

- Earl Nightingale, Co-Founder of Nightingale-Conant

The following article was adapted from the only known interview with Lloyd Conant, a short time before his death on April 2, 1986.

Lloyd, you were a pioneer in the field of putting these types of messages on recorded albums. Did you have doubts that this would really go as a business because no one else was doing it?

Yes, of course. However, we found that the people who bought our products really didn't care whether anyone else ever got them. *They* were pioneers as well and they liked that they had found something new. And the feedback from those people was so great we were encouraged to go ahead. We were dealing with major, forward-looking companies at the time, and they would buy our programs for all their sales force or all their management team. However, when I say "all of their," we were lucky to be selling seven or eight hundred thousand dollars' worth of business in our very best year. We knew we were just scratching the surface, and we were determined to go ahead with it.

We knew that we were on the right track as long as we were selling a product that brought far more value to the end-user than it cost. And we were getting feedback that for every dollar invested in our product, they might be getting back a thousand dollars in return from the ideas that they were gaining. We knew that we, basically, were on the right track and that some day we would be able to figure out a way to reach the greater number of people who could make use of this information. So, we stayed with it.

At first, we had so much in the way of feedback that we thought everyone was excited about this. We actually thought that 100% of the population was interested in this material. Some people would buy two or three hundred of them and just give them out to people in their community. However, we found out the hard way that relatively very few people were interested in what we were doing - most simply couldn't see how to apply the ideas in their life.

I remember we went over to South Bend trying to "save" Studebaker when they were about to close their doors. We found out that was a mistake. They had no budget and they didn't think this way. So, we went over and talked to Oldsmobile, and Oldsmobile bought our products in big numbers because they *did* believe in it. I should point out the obvious, that one of those companies is still in business.

Lloyd, it wasn't so much Nightingale-Conant helping them run their business by telling them how to do that, but it was helping them think about their lives and how they were applying themselves to their business. Is that right?

That's true. In fact we give very little in the way of information. We stimulated them to think positively about reaching greater fulfillment in their lives. Our programs are more or less, as much as the word is not too well understood, motivational, in that they caused the person to motivate himself. We are primarily idea stimulators, or our messages are idea stimulators. We must keep presenting these ideas until we trigger some ideas that you can use.

Even though our customers often want to give us credit for their success, and we can take some credit - but not a whole lot, we simply stimulated them at the right time. But I think most were set to do something big, and we simply came along and helped them over the top. However, because so many of our customers feel a real fellowship with us, it's the most rewarding business that I can imagine.

We feel that if our customers get only one good idea from each of our programs, then we can have a profound influence on their lives. I used to sell business machines, and they were terrific if they could bring the customer a 100% return on the investment in a three-year period. If our programs don't bring 100% return in a month's time, it's a poor investment, which is why we have an unconditional return policy. The last thing we want is for someone to pay for one of our products and not feel that he or she got the best of the deal.

The most beautiful part of it is that if we do inspire great ideas, the customers get to live with those ideas the rest of their lives, and the ideas are going to multiply and grow. So they are bound to have a very profound effect.

Our audio versions can have the most impact because we can learn at times when our hands are busy but our minds are free, such as while driving to work or exercising. Audio learning can save us a half hour or more of dead time every day and keep our minds charged up. We are all blessed with this fabulously poor memory that can forget the bad in our lives, but it can also forget the good. So, we need to be recharged and reminded on a constant basis of the good ideas that we've heard and have forgotten.

A business such as Nightingale- Conant that has endured for nearly half-a-century as a pioneer must have been built on certain bedrock principles. Your programs talk about excellence, success, achievement, and winning, so you've obviously followed some very successful formulas. People not only respect your business, but they respect you as a person. Are there some general rules that you have followed to be a success in business?

Well, there's one rule, the golden rule that almost suffices: If you're treating your customers and associates the way you want to be treated, you've got that situation pretty well taken care of. In *The Science of Getting Rich*, W. D. Wattles wrote that we must always give more in service to our customers and to those around us than we are getting in return. By doing that we are bound to succeed. That little message has had a lasting and profound effect on my life.

It would be no fun to win in a business without our associates winning also. We have always thought about our employees as associates and friends, and by treating everyone as adults and as friends, everything just seems to work.

Consequently, we have had very little turnover. In fact, in the past five years we have had only two people leave us, and one left to get married and move to another part of the world. We try to develop permanent relationships, and it takes something of that nature for someone to leave us.

Our people are often so responsive to the "cause" that they don't want to leave at the end of the day. We do like them to be happy at home as well, but we also like for them to want to come back the next morning. I would hate to think that anyone hated to come to work.

It impressed me the very first time I paid a visit to Nightingale-Conant that you were actually walking around the entire facility saying "hello" to employees, talking to them, and observing some of the things they were doing. Is that part of your management style?

Yes, I feel it's not only necessary, but I enjoy it. I love the interaction with our associates, and I try not to do anything in the office that I can take home. I try to keep all my time during the day available to the customers and associates. I hope that I never "outgrow" that, but I don't know how it could be "growth" to leave it. I think it's a vital part of being a CEO of any company.

Lloyd, The Wall Street Journal several years ago ran a survey of chief officers of companies and what they looked for in young employees or young managers. What do you look for? What are the characteristics of the model of a person working for Nightingale-Conant that you would like to see?

Well, we would like to see, and we do have, veracious people who want to fit into our game plan. We look at the person more than the education. We can tell in a few days how they will make out with us, and we are fortunate in that somehow we seem to attract great people who are eager to grow and to grow with our company.

I think my function is to help each of our associates develop to his or her fullest potential. In some cases, I have a tendency to shelter them too much, but I'm learning to throw bigger and bigger loads on them, and in turn they are then able to develop their own departments and staff.

You often hear the saying, "What's an idea worth?" It's pretty hard to put a price tag on any kind of an idea. A business like ours is based on a big idea. And it takes hundreds, maybe even thousands, of little ideas to keep it afloat. We must each generate several new good ideas every day just to keep the big idea going. I think that's true with most businesses.

Management is an art, not a science, because we're dealing with people - both our customers and our own team here at the office. We are not perfect, but it's something that we must work toward at all times. Each of us on the team is different, yet we all have the same basic drives and desires. So, it's a continuous and very interesting activity to blend all these talents into a team - much like conducting an orchestra.

Running a company like ours is like being the conductor of a great orchestra or symphony in which each person is playing his or her part as definite individuals, with no one person more important than any other, to create the best products and service for our customers. I have always thought of myself as more of a coordinator than a manager, or in staying with the orchestra metaphor, a conductor.

It's always interesting to meet someone who is successful and find out a little bit of the influences that they had in their lives and in their thinking. How would you define success in business? You have obviously been successful in terms of selling programs and meeting certain numerical goals. But I suspect from the answers to the other questions, you define success in a slightly different way.

Success differs with each person. And of course there are so many different areas of our life that you can look at for success: your career, your family and friends, or your contribution to society. There are so many ways to judge success, and each of us has to be his or her own judge as to what success really is.

I used to think that there was a way to "have it made," but now I find out that just doesn't happen - and shouldn't happen. Of course, people do retire; some of them really enjoy it and some do not. You might say that they "have it made," but for me it wouldn't be so. I think we're put here to keep growing and to help other people grow. We must have a dream that's strong enough to carry us through all the petty things that can come up during the long journey toward our vision. Success is in having something worthwhile to be striving toward.

I usually say, "You're not entitled to a big problem until you've solved all those little ones." And so you must be agile to keep looking forward to what's next. Some people succeed at something and then plateau. Then there are others who take that success and parlay it into bigger and bigger successes. As we grow in our profession, at some point we grow into a new plateau. At that point we need to enjoy it for a short time, regroup, and then climb on to the next plateau. And, I think that's the way life *should* be.

I am as charged up today at 70, as I've been at any time in my life. And it's exciting to be in a business where you have that opportunity. We're trying to make that opportunity available for everyone - our associates and our customers. Abraham Lincoln once said that people are just as happy as they want to be, and it is just as true today as it was then. We want to help keep people excited about their work and what they're doing in life.

Of course we need to create a profit along the way, but we know that if our customers are well taken care of, we will get our rewards. It seems like it took a long time for that to start happening, but it's happening now and we're very grateful for it. We feel successful.

Lloyd Conant died shortly after recording this interview, but his dream is ever-present in everything that his company, Nightingale- Conant, touches. Lloyd's son, Vic Conant, continues to lead his company with the same love and devotion to the customers and associates that his father had. And, the goal is still the same: Make possible anyone's ability to live the life he or she most desires.

Chapter 30

Is Your Destination Clear?

People can have anything they want. The trouble is that they don't know what they want. The person who knows what they want knows what they must become, and they then fix their attention on the preparation of themselves toward that end.

Have you ever noticed that ships operate essentially the same way people ought to, but so few do? Maybe you've never given it much thought, but at any given moment, a ship has a direction and a destination. That is, either she's sailing to a predetermined port of call, or she's in port, getting ready to sail to another one. You can ask the captain of any big, far-sailing ship where they're going, and they can tell you instantly - and in one sentence.

How many people do you know who can do the same thing? It seems that most people want too many different things - or at least they think they want them - they're unable to focus their efforts, their minds, and their hearts on anything specific. And all that this leads to is doubt and confusion. They're like the guy who jumped on a horse and rode off in all directions at once. They don't recognize how vital it is to pick one port that's important, then sail to it, rest and refit for a little while, and then sail to another port. In this way, in not so many years, a person can set and reach their goals, one by one, until finally they have a tremendous pile of accomplishments in which to take pride - they have all the things they want, just because they had the sense enough to realize they could do well with only one thing at a time.

There's another analogy that fits here, and maybe it makes the most important point of all. If a ship tied to a dock for some reason had no place to go, she would stay there until she fell apart from rust and disuse. A ship's engine isn't started until she has some place to go. Here again, it's the same with people. This is why it's so important that each of us has a port of call we want to reach - a goal - a place to get to where we feel will be better than the place in which we now find ourselves. If we don't, we might never cast off. We might never start our engines and know the thrill of sailing a charted course to a place we can't see for fully 99 percent of the journey. But we know it's there, and we know that if we keep sailing toward it, we'll reach it.

If someone came up to you today and asked you what your next port of call is - that is, where you are going - could you answer him in one sentence, as could the captain on the bridge of their ship? If not, maybe you'd like to give that some thought.

A clinical Associate Professor of Psychiatry, Dr. Ari Kiev writes, "In my practice as a psychiatrist, I have found that helping people to develop personal goals has proven to be the most effective way to help them cope with problems. Observing the lives of people who have mastered adversity, I have noticed," he writes, "that they have established goals and sought with all their effort to achieve them. From the moment they decided to concentrate all their energies on a specific objective, they began to surmount the most difficult odds."

So writes Dr. Kiev in his book, *A Strategy for Daily Living,* "The establishment of a goal is the key to successful living. And the most important step toward achieving an objective is first to define it." I'm sure you have at least 30 minutes a day in which to list your thoughts about possible goals. Set aside such a period each day for a month. At the end of the time, choose from the possible objectives you have listed, the one that seems most important, and record it separately on a single card. Carry this card with you at all times. Think about this objective every day. Create concrete mental images of the goal, as if you've already accomplished it.

The doctor points out, "You can determine your special talents or strengths in a number of ways, ranging from psychological tests to any analysis of the unexpressed wishes in your dreams. No one method works for everyone." You might start, for example, by clipping and saving magazine and newspaper articles that interest you for 30 days. After which, look for the pervasive trend or trends suggestive of your deep-seated interests and natural strengths. Whenever you discover a strength or talent, think of five possible ways to develop it. Write these strengths down on your card as well, and check it periodically to keep them fresh in your mind.

If possible, have your card laminated and place it on your bathroom mirror so that it is the first and last thoughts of your day. Then focus your day's energy on this goal and on activities that utilize these natural strengths.
Dr. Kiev continues, "Focus on one objective at a time. Like a microchip, the brain, set on a target, will call into play those mental processes that will bring your efforts to fruition. Your actions will conform to your expectations, thereby bringing about the event. If you believe that you will reach your objective, you will continue to work at a task until you have accomplished it."

So, take the advice of the psychiatrist Dr. Ari Kiev and don't be afraid of failure. As Herodotus wrote, "It is better by noble boldness to run the risk of being subject to half of the evils we anticipate than to remain in cowardly listlessness for fear of what may happen. "

Sit down and make a list of everything you want in life. When you do this, you will make some surprising discoveries. You might find that you have already managed to get many of the things you have wanted seriously. Or, if you don't have most or all of them, chances are you are now in the process of getting them. If your list contains some items you want very much but do not have, you might ask yourself why you have failed to get them. Chances are that you have not tried very hard. Or perhaps you felt, for one reason or another, that these things are completely beyond your ability to achieve. These wants make very worthwhile goals.

It's a good idea to have two lists of things you want. The first list would include those bigger goals that relate to your career or the overall good of your life or your family. These might include the position and/or income you are working toward, perhaps a higher educational degree, a certain amount of money in savings, a goal of height of business success, or that beautiful home you have had your eye on.

The other list could be a fun list. It might include the car you want for no good reason except it's the car you happen to want, redecorating your house, getting new furniture, traveling to some special place - perhaps abroad - or buying a new wardrobe. This is a list of things you want just because you want them.

You should have long-range goals. These should be on your number one list, and each of them should be numbered in the order of importance to you. These are goals that might take five years or longer to achieve. They're extremely worthwhile, and you should be working toward them daily. These are the

133

goals that give meaning and direction and substance to your life.

But you also need short-range goals. These are the goals that add zest and interest to your life and break up the monotony of the long haul for the long-range goals.

If you're honest with yourself about the things you want - not idle wishes that change from day to day but things you are serious about - you'll find that they all can be yours, and in a surprisingly short time, if they are taken one at a time.

It's been said, "People can have anything they want. The trouble is that they don't know what they want. " Get off by yourself for a quiet hour or two, and make up your card and your two lists. It is a fun and rewarding exercise and will prove to be the first step toward living the life you most desire.

The great historical philosophers, teachers and prophets all agreed...

"You become what you think about" - Earl Nightingale
"A man's life is what his thoughts make of it." - Emperor Marcus Aurelius
"A man is what he thinks about all day long." - Ralph Waldo Emerson

Do you appreciate the life you have fashioned for yourself?
When was the last time you assessed your long-term goals?
Are you prepared to create new goals after you have accomplished your current goals?

A man hunting tigers in India was suddenly surprised by a huge Bengal tiger - it was almost on top of him. The man raised his rifle and fired, but he overshot and missed. The tiger, frightened by the man and thrown off stride by the noise of the gun, leaped toward the hunter but the leap was too wide, and he missed his prey.

The man returned to camp and spent several hours perfecting his aim for short distances and quick firing. On the following day, he again stalked the tiger. Finally, he spotted the beast at some distance - practicing short leaps.

What are your goals?

Chapter 31

What Happens When You Run Out of Goals?

Here are some interesting questions you might want to try answering. One: If you could completely change places with any other person in the world, would you do it? And who would that person be? Two: If you could work at any job you could choose, would that work be different from the work you're doing now? Three: If you could live in any part of the country you want to live in, would you move from where you are now living? Four: If you could go back to age 12 and live your life from that point over again, would you do it?

Studies indicate that the great majority of people, even though they have a certain amount of dissatisfaction with their present lives and don't seem to be as happy as they might be, will answer "no" to all four questions. A person often feels when he's accomplished everything he's worked and struggled for so long to achieve, he finds himself depressed more and more of the time. He has a fine job and an excellent income, a beautiful home, a wonderful spouse and children. In fact, everything is finally just as he'd planned it for so many years. And for no reason that he can put his finger on, all the fun and enthusiasm has strongly disappeared. He's listless and unhappy, and he can't think of a single reason why.

This has become a common modern malady, especially in retirement, and it's what so often happens when a person runs out of goals. This is when the game of life begins to go to pot, and the person needs to remind himself of the basic rules for successful, enthusiastic living. And the first rule is that a human being must have something worthwhile toward which he's working. Without that, everything else, even the most remarkable achievements of the past and all the trappings of worldly success tend to turn sour. Achieving our life goals can be compared to opening our presents on Christmas morning and watching those we love open theirs. We look forward to the day, plan, and work toward it. Suddenly it is there and all of the presents have been opened, and then what?

Well, we must then turn our thoughts and attention to other things. The successful novelist begins planning his next book before he completes the one he's working on. The scientist always has something new and challenging to turn to when he completes a project. The teacher has a new class coming up. The young family has children to raise and get through school, the new home to buy, the promotion to work for.

But for millions who reach their 40s and 50s and find they've done all they set out to do and that there are no new challenges to give them stimulus and direction, there often comes the most trying time of their lives - the search for meaning, for new meaning, and it must be found if the old interest and vitality are to be restored to their lives, if they're to achieve renewal as persons.

If you understand this, even the search for new meaning can bring new interest into your life. You've got to say to yourself, "All right, I've done what I've set out to do. Now I must find something new and interesting to do."

Chapter 32

Napoleon Hill's Think and Grow Rich

Napoleon Hill has arguably influenced the success of more men and women than any other person in history.

Born in a one-room cabin, he began his career as a journalist. His big break came when he was asked to interview steel-magnate Andrew Carnegie. Carnegie was so impressed with the young reporter that he convinced Hill to research and organize the world's first philosophy of individual achievement.

All over the free world, there are thousands of successful men and women who are where they are today because they once picked up a copy of *Think and Grow Rich* by Napoleon Hill. Without question, this single book has had a greater influence on the lives, accomplishments, and fortunes of more people than any other work of its kind.

This remarkable book helped me decide once and for all how I was to accomplish my goal. It unified my thinking and gave me a straight, clear road to the point I decided to reach. One of my closest friends found the book, stayed home for three days reading and digesting its material, and he then went on to reach the top of his industry. I've sat in richly paneled executive offices and listened to world-famous business leaders tell me how reading *Think and Grow Rich* changed their lives.

When the last page of *Think and Grow Rich* is read, the hand that puts the book down on the table is a different hand. The man who then stands up and walks out into the world is a different, a changed man - the possessor of the unique knowledge that will enable him to turn dreams into reality, thoughts into things. So-called fate and exterior circumstances are no longer in command. He who had been a passenger is now suddenly the captain.

The secret behind *Think and Grow Rich,* the reason why it has withstood the test of time, is because it stands on the foundation of truth: the clear, unchallengeable fact that everything begins with an idea. One may start with nothing but ideas, but ideas are incredibly powerful when they're supported by Definiteness of Purpose, persistence, and a burning desire for their translation into material objects or riches - "riches" being whatever it is you happen to want.

In other words, by controlling your mind, you can control your destiny. And you can start that amazing process today, by absorbing and applying Napoleon Hill's famous 13 principles for unbridled success.

Desire

Desire is the starting point for all achievement, the first step toward riches. But it's here that we so often run into a roadblock. A person will say, "I know what I desire, but can I get it?"

The answer was best expressed by Emerson: "There's nothing capricious in nature, and the implanting of a desire indicates that its gratification is in the constitution of the creature that feels it." In other words, you would not have the desire unless you were capable of its achievement.

Your burning desire is nothing more than an accurate picture of what you will one day become. So right here, firmly establish in your mind that which you desire more than anything else, and cherish and nurture that desire. Do not suppress or annihilate it. A man without desire has within him no principle of action, nor motive to act.

Faith

Faith is the state of mind that may be induced or created by affirmation or repeated instructions to the subconscious mind by conscious auto-suggestion. By summoning over and over again a mental image of yourself already having accomplished your main desire, you will muster the faith you need. Faith is vital to accomplishment.

Have faith that you can accomplish that which you seek, for you would never have decided upon it unless it was meant for you to accomplish it. If you find it difficult at times to have faith in yourself, you may be certain that you can have faith in these principles.

Auto Suggestion

Through repeated suggestion, the subconscious mind can be put to work for you. It's the faculty of being able to concentrate your mind on your burning desire until your subconscious mind accepts it as fact and begins to devise ways of bringing it about. Here's where hunches come from, sudden flashes of thought, inspiration, or guidance.

To access the power of auto suggestion, go into some quiet spot, perhaps in bed at night. Close your eyes and repeat aloud so you may hear your own words a careful reaffirmation of whatever your goal happens to be. If it's the accumulation of a sum of money, reiterate the time limit for its accumulation and a description of the service or merchandise you intend to give in return for it. As you carry out these instructions, see yourself already in possession of your goal.

Specialized Knowledge

Knowledge is power only to the extent that it's organized into a definite plan of action and directed to a definite end. Before you can be sure of your ability to transmute desire into its monetary equivalent, you will require specialized knowledge of the service, merchandise, or profession that you intend to offer in return for fortune.

Realize that you must learn all you can about your specialty. Set aside a definite time every day for learning more about what it is you do for a living. Take the courses that are offered on your subject and associate with people who know your business well.

Imagination

Whatever the mind of man can conceive and believe, it can achieve. Man's only limitation, within reason, lies in the development and use of his imagination and subsequent motivation to action. The great leaders of business, industry, and finance, and the great artists, musicians, poets, and writers became great because they developed the power of self-motivation.

As you go about your daily work, think constantly of ways in which it could be done better, more efficiently. Think of the changes that are inevitable. Can they be made now? If you feel limited, remember the words of the late Frank Lloyd Wright: "The human race built most nobly when limitations were greatest and, therefore, when most was required of imagination in order to build at all."

Decision

Analysis of several hundred people who've accumulated fortunes well beyond the million-dollar mark disclose the fact that every one of them had the habit of reaching decisions promptly and of changing these decisions slowly, if and when they were changed.

When you make up your mind, stay with it. The majority of people who fail are generally easily influenced by the opinions of others. Opinions are the cheapest commodities on earth. Keep your own counsel when you begin to put into practice the principles described here by reaching your own decisions and following them. Take no one into your confidence except the members of your mastermind alliance (as discussed later), and be very careful in your selection of this group, choosing only those who will be in complete sympathy and harmony with your purpose. Close friends and relatives, while not meaning to do so, often handicap one through uninformed opinions and sometimes through ridicule.

Persistence

Persistence is simply the power of will. Willpower and desire, when properly combined, make an irresistible pair. Persistence is to an individual what carbon is to steel. In uncounted thousands of cases, persistence has stood as the difference between success and failure. It is the lack of this quality more than any other that keeps the majority from great accomplishment. As soon as the going gets tough, they fold.

If you're to accomplish the goal you set for yourself, you must form the habit of persistence. Things will get difficult. It will seem as though there's no longer any reason to continue. Everything in you will tell you to give up, to quit trying. It is right here that if you'll go that extra mile and keep going, the skies will clear and you'll begin to see the first signs of the abundance that is to be yours because you had the courage to persist. With persistence will come success.

Enthusiastic Support

It is of great significance that behind practically every great leader has been the supportive love and inspiration of a spouse. When things get tough - and you can count on it, they will - you may be deserted by some you thought were friends. But if you've got a good woman or man supporting you, you will never be alone. He or she will be willing to start over again if necessary and will give you the new enthusiasm that comes through faith in you.

Having someone to love is having someone to share your success and
Accomplishments, to give you the praise that all of us need from time to time. A person can become successful without a spouse and family, but much of the real joy is lost if it cannot be shared. Take care of your spouse and children as your greatest possessions.

Organized Planning

The first of the six steps for transforming desire into reality is the formation of a definite, practical plan through which this transformation may be made (see From Desire to Reality in Six Easy Steps). Once you do, it is critical that you ally yourself with one or more people or a group of as many people as you may need for the creation and carrying out of your plan. These people are your "mastermind alliance."

Before forming your mastermind alliance, decide what advantages and benefits you may offer the individual members of your group in return for their cooperation. No one will work indefinitely without compensation, though this may not always be in the form of money.

Arrange to meet with the members of your mastermind alliance at least twice a week, and more often if possible, until you have jointly perfected the necessary plan or plans for the accomplishment of your goal.

Maintain perfect harmony between yourself and every member of your mastermind alliance. Keep in mind these facts: First, you are engaged in an undertaking of major importance to you. To be sure of success, you must have plans that are as faultless as possible. Second, you must have the advantage of the experience, education, native ability, and imagination of other minds. This is in harmony with the methods followed by every person who has risen above the average. Work at this until you have a well-executed formal plan for reaching your objective. In this way you're never confused or wondering what you should do next. Every morning you know exactly what you're going to do and why.

Organized planning is one the most important principles, because a person without a plan is like a ship without a course. With no place to go, disaster is a probability.

The Power of the Mastermind

No two minds ever come together without thereby creating a third - a third invisible, intangible force that may be likened to a third mind. You may have noticed many times that by discussing something with another person you suddenly get good ideas as a result of the discussion, ideas you would not have gotten without this association. Well, the same thing happens to the other person. A lot of good ideas have been born in individual minds as a result of having met in committee.

Associating with your mastermind alliance is not meant as a means of letting others do your thinking for you, far from it. It is meant to stimulate your own thinking through the association with other minds. No one knows everything. The more sympathetic minds you get together - that is, minds working for a common purpose - the more related information is going to be available. Great ideas are a combination of related information.

Pick the members of your mastermind group with care. Make sure they're people you respect and who are hard working and conscientious. You'll have a lot of fun, and you'll reach your goals just that much sooner.

The Subconscious Mind

The subconscious mind is a mental area in which all inputs through any of the five senses are classified and recorded, and from which they may be recalled or withdrawn like data from the storage banks of a limitless computer. No one knows very much about what we call the subconscious mind but we do know that it is incalculably powerful and can solve our problems if we go about using it the right way.

The best way is to hold in your conscious mind as often as possible a clear picture of yourself already having accomplished your goal. Know what you want. Define it clearly, and then project it on the motion picture screen of your mind. Hold it. See yourself doing and having the things you have when your objective will have been reached. Do this as often as practical, particularly at night just before you go to sleep and the first thing upon waking. As you do this, your subconscious will begin to lead you toward your objective. Don't fight it. Follow your sudden hunches, the ideas that come into your mind, knowing that they may well represent subconscious knowledge.

If you'll keep at this, you'll be amazed and delighted by the ideas that just seem to come from nowhere.

The Power of the Brain

If you had access to all the wealth in the world and used only a penny, you would be doing exactly what most of us very probably have been doing in the use of our brains.

You own in your brain the most marvelous, miraculous, inconceivably powerful force the world has ever known.

It is the brain that has given us the computer, supersonic airplane, our deep rocket probes into outer space, the sciences, and the arts. All of what we know today and will achieve tomorrow is born from this small, gray mass each of us carries around.

Can you doubt, even for a moment, that your brain can bring you and yours everything you want here on earth? Recognize its power, give it the job you've decided to accomplish, and watch it handle it.

The Sixth Sense

The sixth sense can be described as the sense through which your infinite intelligence may and will communicate. This principle is the apex of the philosophy. It can be assimilated, understood, and applied only by first mastering the other 12 principles.

The sixth sense is that function of the subconscious mind that has been referred to as the creative imagination. It's also been referred to as the receiving set through which ideas flash into the mind, sometimes called hunches or inspirations. The sixth sense cannot be described to a person who has not mastered the other principles of this philosophy, because such a person has no knowledge and no experience to serve as points of reference. The sixth sense is not something one can take off and put on at will. The ability to use this great power comes slowly through application of the other principles we've outlined. So begin to develop it now by applying the principles we've talked about here.

Remember this: Man can create nothing that he does not first conceive in the form of an idea, a desire. Keep fear out of your mind. Concentrate on the mental picture of yourself achieving your desire. Cut yourself away from the average - from the mediocre - and chart your course on the dream in your heart. These 13 principles will never let you down. You need only remember and use them.

From Desire to Reality in Six Easy Steps

Six definite practical steps to transform a burning desire into reality.

1. Fix in your mind an exact picture of what you desire. It's not sufficient merely to say, for example, "I want plenty of money." Be definite as to the amount.
2. Determine exactly what you intend to give in return for the thing you desire. There's no such reality as something for nothing.
3. Establish a definite date by which you intend to possess the desired thing.
4. Create a definite plan for carrying out your desire and begin at once, whether you feel entirely ready or not to put this plan into action.
5. Write out a clear, concise statement of your responses to the preceding four steps.
6. Read your written statement aloud twice daily. Once after arising in the morning and once just before retiring at night. As you read, see and feel and believe yourself already in possession of whatever your goal happens to be.

"Through some strange and powerful principle of mental chemistry, nature wraps up in the impulse [of a] strong desire that something which recognizes no such word as impossible and accepts no such reality as failure."
- Napoleon Hill

The Genius behind Napoleon Hill's Science of Personal Achievement

These are just a few of the influential people Napoleon Hill interviewed on his 20-year quest to discover the science behind success.

Henry Ford - Founder of Ford Motor Co.
Theodore Roosevelt - President of the United States
Charles M. Schwab - President of United States Steel Corp.
John D. Rockefeller - Founder of Standard Oil Companies
Thomas A. Edison - Inventor
F. W. Woolworth - Founder of F. W. Woolworth Co.
Woodrow Wilson - President of the United States
Wm. Howard Taft - President of the United States
J. Pierpont Morgan Sr. - Builder of "The House of Morgan"
Harvey S. Firestone - Founder of Firestone Tire & Rubber Co.
Wm. Wrigley Jr.- Founder of Wm. Wrigley Jr. Co.
Julius Rosenwald - Chairman of Board, Sears, Roebuck & Co.

Chapter 33

How to Give a Great Speech

Congratulations if you are already an accomplished presenter; you are in an elite minority. For the rest of us, the prospect of having to give a speech can feel like the terminal stages of some kind of tropical fever. Fortunately, there are secrets that anyone can leverage to make a great speech. You may even learn to enjoy it!

There are two kinds of public speakers: There are those who are asked to talk to a group and those who, because of their position, are forced to talk before groups - people such as ministers, teachers, executives, and sales managers.

In the first instance - that is, if you're asked to make a speech - it means you know something others want to hear. It usually means you're an expert on some subject, and so people come to hear you because they want to. If your job demands that you talk before groups, you have an even greater responsibility because your audience must listen to you whether they like it or not.

But in either case, you can make a good speech with a little preparation. Here are some guidelines.

A good speech is like good conversation

A good conversationalist will make a good speaker. He's sensitive to the presence of others. His antennae are forever alert, picking up signals from his audience and involving them in his talk.

Good conversation is one of the great joys of human commerce. Good conversation should be like the game of tennis, in which the ball is struck back and forth, with each player participating equally. Bores are like golfers who just keep hitting their own ball, over and over and over again.

A good speaker is able to achieve a marvelous give-and-take with her audience, just as a good conversationalist does with the person she's with. She recognizes that people in our society desire recognition more than any other factor.

She will ask her audience questions such as, "Do you agree with that?" Then she'll pause and read their response - by their silence, their attention, their nods, their poking of the person sitting next to them, by their laughter, or by their seriousness at the right places. If they're bored, they'll find ways of showing it, despite their best efforts. If they're interested, they'll show that too. And we have a duty to be interesting or we shouldn't get up there in the first place. That is the task of the speaker, whether we're the manager of the sales force, in a car dealership, an insurance agency, real estate office, or a large international organization. When interest leaves, the sell goes out of our message.

Our responsibility is not only to create a speech that will lead an audience to a believable conclusion; we must also make the very building blocks of that conclusion as fascinating as we can. It is in this way that we can hold the attention of our audience until we get to that all-important final point. In addition, if we can develop techniques that make our audience feel that we are conversing with them, we will convey that we care what they are thinking - and that will create the emotional climate for them to accept us as favorably as possible.

The single-theme formula

Professional salespeople, marketing experts, and leaders in the advertising profession know the importance of selling one thing at a time. Only catalogs can successfully handle a multitude of items. In a five-minute speech or even a long speech, it's important to have a single theme, and, like a good salesperson, you pose the problem and then give your solution. At the end, the problem is restated and the solution quickly summarized.

Your opening statement should be an attention getter. For example, you might say, "Scientists all over the world are agreed that the world's oceans are dying." A sobering thought indeed. It captures immediate interest, and everyone is thinking, "Why, that would presage the end of the world. What are we doing about it?"

Using an internationally recognized authority as your reference, someone such as Jacques Cousteau, you provide the supporting evidence that your opening remark is indeed true, and then you proceed to outline the possible ways that the disaster might be averted. At the end, you might say, "Yes, the oceans of the world are dying today, but if we can marshal the combined efforts of the world's peoples, if we can influence every maritime country to pass laws governing the pollution of the seas by oil tankers..." So you end on a note of hope and at the same time enlist the sympathy of every one of your listeners in your cause.

Not all talks are about social problems, of course. You might be talking about a recent fishing trip, in which case, you find something of special interest in the story and open with that. You might say "Ounce for ounce, the rainbow trout is one of the gamest fish on earth." It's a much better attention getter and interest stimulator than saying, "I want to tell you about my recent fishing trip." A few words about the fish you were after, and then you can work in the rest. "Two weeks ago, John Cooper and I decided to try our luck on the White River near Carter, Arkansas. It's one of the most naturally beautiful spots in the country" and so on. Stay with the trip and that rainbow trout, the hero of your story, and how good it tasted cooked over an open fire on the bank of the river. Then at the close, to more closely link your listeners to the subject, you might say, "If you've never been trout fishing, let me recommend it as one of the world's best ways to forget your problems, clear your brain, and gain a new perspective. And when you hook a rainbow trout, you're in for one of the greatest thrills of a lifetime. "

Watch your personal pronouns. Keep yourself out of your conversation as much as possible. As with the case of the fishing story, talk about the fish, the beautiful scenery, and your companions, other people you met, a humorous incident or two perhaps, but don't keep saying, " I did this" and "I did that." The purpose of the speech is not to talk about you but rather the subject matter. There's an old saying that *small minds talk about things, average minds talk about people, and great minds talk about ideas.* What you're selling is almost always an idea, even if it's painting the house. The idea is the good appearance or the protection of the house. The fishing trip story is about the idea of getting away and going after exciting game fish. *One idea, well developed, is the key.*

Just as a beautiful painting is put together by a thousand brush strokes, each stroke makes a contribution to the main theme, the overall picture. And it's the same with a good speech.

Don't be a comedian

Humor isn't something that can be forced, nor should it be reached for. It's something that comes naturally to those with the ability, or at least it seems to. If you have it, congratulations. Use it wisely. If you don't have it, use it sparingly and make certain it's really funny before you use it at all. Don't try to dabble in one of the most difficult professions in the world - that of a stand-up comedian.

Before you include a joke in your speech, ask yourself this: Why am I telling it? Jokes aren't *necessary* to the opening of a speech. Neither are funny comments, unless they have a clever tie-in of some sort that the audience will genuinely appreciate and enjoy.

I've heard so many tedious speakers say, following the introduction, "That reminds me of a story..." and then proceed to tell a story that hasn't the faintest resemblance to anything said in the introduction at all. It didn't remind him. He just wanted to tell a joke, and everybody in the audience knows it and begins to move their feet and cough and look around for the exit.

Here's a good rule to follow that I've found works. If there is any doubt in your mind whatever, if there is the faintest feeling of uneasiness about a story, never tell it. That feeling of uneasiness is your more intelligent subconscious trying to tell you to forget it. Save if for the locker room at the club if you must tell it.

If you want a foolproof system, use the enormously successful Jack Benny system: Make yourself the joke. Benny has produced the most prolonged, helpless laughter in the history of show business. It happened on his old radio program when he was approached by a robber who said, "Your money or your life." What followed was simply silence, the deadly, convulsively funny silence that only Jack Benny could manage. The silence lasted only a few seconds when the laughter began, then mounted and mounted and continued for a record-breaking period of time, I think something like 15 minutes. Finally, when it did subside, the robber repeated, "I said your money or your life." And Jack Benny replied, "I'm thinking. I'm thinking."

Again the laughter took hold and the program nearly ran out of time before it could even attempt to finish. A simple silence did it as Jack tried desperately to decide which was more important to him, his money or his life. He was always the loser in his elaborate plans, as is the coyote in his attempts to trap the roadrunner. People love us when we're foiled by our own weaknesses.

If humor is your forte, then you don't need any advice or help from me. If it isn't, use it sparingly and in good taste. It's wonderful when it's right. It's so awful when it isn't.

Speak with style

I was a speaker at a hospital benefit, and as I waited in the wings of a large theater where the benefit was being staged, I noticed that one of the officials for the evening was on stage in front of the lectern reading the names of the various high school graduates from the community who had won scholarships in nursing. He never looked up at the audience. He spoke in such low monotones that he was difficult to hear, even with an excellent audio system, and his performance was as lackluster as any I've ever seen. When he was through, he walked back to where I was standing in the wings. As he disappeared from view to the audience, his face broke with a beautiful broad smile, and he said in a strong voice, "Man, am I glad that's over." I stopped him and I said, "You should have flashed that wonderful smile to the audience and used your normal voice. It's excellent." "Oh, that," he shuddered. "I'm scared to death out there. "

Now, the audience got a picture of a very lackluster man with no personality and no style whatsoever, a total cipher. Yet, here was a good-looking man with a beautiful smile, an excellent style of his own that his friends and acquaintances no doubt greatly admired. I wanted to go on stage and say to that great audience. "I wish you could see so-and-so as he really is. He's quite a guy."

Everyone has his or her own special style. It seems to come with the genes and the upbringing and the education, all of thousands of experiences that coalesce to form a person's own unique style.

You have only to study prominent people on television to quickly see that each of them has a style all his or her own that he or she is completely unconscious of. Just as we should never doubt our hunches or our own unique powers, we should never doubt that we have a natural style. If, and it's a big if - if we can be natural.

The key is to lose ourselves in our material. In an ideal speech, we are conscious of putting on a performance, but at the same time we're so interested in what we're talking about and we know our subject so thoroughly, we can immerse ourselves in it.

I was chatting with a salesman on an airplane one time. It turned out we were both going to the same convention. I had to speak. He had to receive his company's highest honor as national sales leader. As our conversation grew more animated, I asked him the secret of being number one in sales with his company. And he gave me the most interesting answer. He said, "I was in this business for several years, and I tried hard and I worked hard, but I was a long way from the top. Then one day, a wonderful thing happened. All of a sudden, things were turned around. Instead of my being in this business, the business got into me."

He looked at me and his eyes were shining, and he asked, "Do you know what I mean?" I told him I knew exactly what he meant and he could number himself among the most fortunate human beings on earth, the people who actually enjoy what they're doing, the real stars. It reminded me of John Stuart Mill's theory of happiness in his book *Utilitarianism*. He said that only those people who do not seek happiness *directly* are happy. People who spend their time helping others and are engaged in some art or pursuit - followed not by a means, but as itself an ideal end - find happiness along the way. The important part is that those who are the happiest are engaged in a daily pursuit, followed not just as a means, but as itself an ideal end. And it's the same in making a fine speech.

Unless the speech is in us to the extent that we can forget ourselves to a degree, it will never carry the impelling, moving effect of a great speech, the kind that brings the audience to its feet at the end of it.

I'll never forget as a youngster hearing Franklin D. Roosevelt say in a campaign speech in that high, stentorian, and effective voice, "We must prevent the princes of privilege from dominating this great country." I remember so vividly the beautiful alliteration "prevent the princes of privilege." Alliteration sticks in the mind, as does short poetry. At one time earlier in our culture, virtually all oral traditions, passed from one generation to another, were in a kind of poetry because it was easier to remember. How can we ever forget "Mary had a little lamb" or "Thirty days hath September, April, June, and November"? Or how about powerful onomatopoeia such as "The stock market hit bottom with an ominous thud"?

Well, perhaps I could have thought of a more cheerful example, but there is poetry in the proper use of words. We hear so many bad speeches, a good one is like a cool green oasis in a burning desert. A good, but unaffected style helps.

They laughed when I stood up to talk

My friend Norm Guess, formerly of the Dartnell Company in Chicago, sent me a little piece on some of the causes of our fears of groups... and how to overcome them.

1. The fear of self: Just plain self-consciousness, a feeling that expresses itself in the mental question, "What in blazes am I doing this for? How in the world did I get myself into this situation?"

2. Reflections from the past. The remembrance, even subliminally, of old classroom failures; being laughed at or ridiculed.

3. Over concern about what others think. The questioning of our authority to be talking before such a group.

4. Poor preparation. The panicky feeling that the speech needs work or complete overhauling or throwing away.

5. Lack of courage to try new things. The fear of doing the unusual.

6. Lack of encouragement from others. I know it always helps me tremendously to hear a comment such as, "The group is looking forward to hearing what you have to say."

Well, what do you do about these problems?

• Recognize that others have the same fear.
• Try to analyze what and why you fear.
• Find a compulsion to speak; realize that you have important things to say and that you want to say them.
• Be prepared.
• Take a course; join Toastmasters.
• There's nothing like actually doing it.
• Talk only on subjects you know very well, subjects you're an expert on and feel comfortable with.

Someone has said, "The human mind is a wonderful thing. It begins at birth and never stops until you get the chance to say something before a group of people." Turn the situation around; realize that if you were in the audience, you'd be interested in what you have to say.

BN Publishing
Improving People's Life

www.bnpublishing.net

Recommended Readings

•Technical Analysis of Stock Trends, Robert D. Edwards, John Magee, www.bnpublishing.net

•Wall Street: The Other Las Vegas, Nicolas Darvas, www.bnpublishing.net

•The Anatomy of Success, Nicolas Darvas, www.bnpublishing.net

• The Dale Carnegie Course on Effective Speaking, Personality Development, and the Art of How to Win Friends & Influence People, Dale Carnegie, www.bnpublishing.net

• The Law of Success In Sixteen Lessons by Napoleon Hill (Complete, Unabridged), Napoleon Hill, www.bnpublishing.net

• It Works, R. H. Jarrett, www.bnpublishing.net

•Darvas System for Over the Counter Profits, Nicolas Darvas, www.bnpublishing.net

• The Art of Public Speaking (Audio CD), Dale Carnegie, wwww.bnpublishing.net

• The Success System That Never Fails (Audio CD), W. Clement Stone, www.bnpublishing.net